THE THEATRE OF TENNESSEE WILLIAMS

Volume VI

By TENNESSEE WILLIAMS

THE THEATRE OF TENNESSEE WILLIAMS

Volume VI

27 Wagons Full of Cotton
and Other Short Plays

A NEW DIRECTIONS BOOK

Manufactured in the United States of America
New Directions Books are printed on acid-free paper.
First published clothbound by New Directions in 1981 (ISBN 0-8112-0794-3) and as New Directions Paperbook 748 in 1992.
Published simultaneously in Canada by Penguin Books Canada Limited

Library of Congress Cataloging-in-Publication Data

(Revised for vol. 6)

Williams, Tennessee, 1911-1983.
  The theatre of Tennessee Williams.
    (v. 3: A New Directions paperbook ; 736)
    Contents: v. 1. Battle of the angels. The glass menagerie. A streetcar named Desire—v. 2. The eccentricities of a nightingale. Summer and smoke. The rose tattoo. Camino Real—   —[etc.]—v. 6. 27 wagons full of cotton and other short plays.
PS3545.I5365A19   1990   812'.54   90-5998
ISBN 0-8112-1215-7 (v. 6 : pbk. : alk. paper)

New Directions Books are published for James Laughlin
by New Directions Publishing Corporation,
80 Eighth Avenue, New York 10011

SECOND PRINTING

ACKNOWLEDGMENTS

Most of the plays included in *The Theatre of Tennessee Williams, Vol. VI* were first published in 1945 as *27 Wagons Full of Cotton and Other One-Act Plays;* two plays ("Something Unspoken" and "Talk to Me Like the Rain") were added in 1953 and that edition was subsequently issued as New Directions Paperbook 217 in 1966. To the expanded collection three plays have been added: *The Unsatisfactory Supper* (first published with the screenplay for *Baby Doll* in 1956); *Steps Must Be Gentle* (first published in a limited edition by William Targ in 1980); and *The Demolition Downtown* (first published in *Esquire* in 1971).

Excerpts from Hart Crane's "Chaplinesque" (used as an epigraph to *The Strangest Kind of Romance*) and "The Broken Tower" (quoted in *Steps Must Be Gentle*) are reprinted from *The Collected Poems of Hart Crane* (Copyright 1933 by Liveright Publishing Corporation) by permission of W. W. Norton & Company, Inc.

Contents

27 WAGONS FULL OF COTTON

A Mississippi Delta Comedy

Now Eros shakes my soul, a wind on the mountain, falling on the oaks.

SAPPHO

CHARACTERS

JAKE MEIGHAN, a cotton-gin owner

FLORA MEIGHAN, his wife

SILVA VICARRO, superintendent of the Syndicate Plantation

The scene is the front porch of the Meighans' cottage near Blue Mountain, Mississippi. The porch is narrow and rises into a single narrow gable. There are spindling white pillars on either side supporting the porch roof and a door of Gothic design and two Gothic windows on either side of it. The peaked door has an oval of richly stained glass, azure, crimson, emerald, and gold. At the windows are fluffy white curtains gathered coquettishly in the middle of baby-blue satin bows. The effect is not unlike a doll's house.

It is early evening and there is a faint rosy dusk in the sky. Shortly after the curtain rises, Jake Meighan, a fat man of sixty, scrambles out the front door and races around the corner of the house carrying a gallon can of coal oil. A dog barks at him. A car is heard starting and receding rapidly in the distance. A moment later Flora calls from inside the house.

FLORA: Jake! I've lost m' white kid purse! [*Closer to the door*] Jake? Look'n see 'f uh laid it on th' swing. [*There is a pause.*] Guess I could've left it in th' Chevy? [*She comes up to screen door.*] Jake. Look'n see if uh left it in th' Chevy. Jake? [*She steps outside in the fading rosy dusk. She switches on the porch light and stares about, slapping at gnats attracted by the light. Locusts provide the only answering voice. Flora gives a long nasal call.*] Ja-ay—a-a-ake! [*A cow moos in the distance with the same inflection. There is a muffled explosion somewhere about half a mile away. A strange flickering glow appears, the reflection of a burst of flame. Distant voices are heard exclaiming.*]

VOICES [*shrill, cackling like hens*]:
You heah that noise?
Yeah! Sound like a bomb went off!
Oh, look!
Why, it's a fire!
Where's it at? You tell?

Th' Syndicate Plantation!
Oh, my God! Let's go! [*A fire whistle sounds in the distance.*]
Henry! Start th' car! You all wanta go with us?
Yeah, we'll be right out!
Hurry, honey! [*A car can be heard starting up.*]
Be right there!
Well, hurry.

VOICE [*just across the dirt road*]: Missus Meighan?

FLORA: Ye-ah?

VOICE: Ahn't you goin' th' fire?

FLORA: I wish I could but Jake's gone off in th' Chevy.

VOICE: Come awn an' go with us, honey!

FLORA: Oh, I cain't an' leave th' house wide open! Jake's gone off with th' keys. What do you all think it is on fire?

VOICE: Th' Syndicate Plantation!

FLORA: Th' Syndicate Plan-*ta*-tion? [*The car starts off and recedes.*] Oh, my Go-od! [*She climbs laboriously back up on the porch and sits on the swing which faces the front. She speaks tragically to herself.*] Nobody! Nobody! Never! Never! Nobody! [*Locusts can be heard. A car is heard approaching and stopping at a distance back of house. After a moment Jake ambles casually up around the side of the house.*]

FLORA [*in a petulant babyish tone*]: Well!

JAKE: Whatsamatter, Baby?

FLORA: I never known a human being could be that mean an' thoughtless!

4

JAKE: Aw, now, that's a mighty broad statement fo' you to make, Mrs. Meighan. What's the complaint this time?

FLORA: Just flew out of the house without even sayin' a word!

JAKE: What's so bad about that?

FLORA: I told you I had a headache comin' on an' had to have a dope, there wassen a single bottle lef' in th' house, an' you said, Yeah, get into yuh things 'n' we'll drive in town right away! So I get into m' things an' I cain't find m' white kid purse. Then I remember I left it on th' front seat of th' Chevy. I come out here t' git it. Where are you? Gone off! Without a word! Then there's a big explosion! Feel my heart!

JAKE: Feel my baby's heart? [*He puts a hand on her huge bosom.*]

FLORA: Yeah, just you feel it, poundin' like a hammer! How'd I know what happened? You not here, just disappeared somewhere!

JAKE [*sharply*]: Shut up! [*He pushes her head roughly.*]

FLORA: Jake! What did you do that fo'?

JAKE: I don't like how you holler! Holler ev'rything you say!

FLORA: What's the matter with you?

JAKE: Nothing's the matter with me.

FLORA: Well, why did you go off?

JAKE: I didn' go off!

5

FLORA: You certainly *did* go off! Try an' tell me that you never went off when I just now seen an' heard you drivin' back in th' car? What uh you take me faw? No sense a-tall?

JAKE: If you got sense you keep your big mouth shut!

FLORA: Don't talk to me like that!

JAKE: Come on inside.

FLORA: I won't. Selfish an' inconsiderate, that's what you are! I told you at supper, There's not a bottle of Coca-Cola left on th' place. You said, Okay, right after supper we'll drive on over to th' White Star drugstore an' lay in a good supply. When I come out of th' house—

JAKE [*standing in front of her and gripping her neck with both hands*]: Look here! Listen to what I tell you!

FLORA: *Jake!*

JAKE: Shhh! Just listen, Baby.

FLORA: Lemme go! G'damn you, le' go my throat!

JAKE: Jus' try an' concentrate on what I tell yuh!

FLORA: Tell me what?

JAKE: I ain't been off th' po'ch.

FLORA: Huh!

JAKE: I ain't been off th' front po'ch! Not since supper! Understand that, now?

6

FLORA: Jake, honey, you've gone out of you' mind!

JAKE: Maybe so. Never you mind. Just get that straight an' keep it in your haid. I ain't been off the porch of this house since supper.

FLORA: But you sure as God *was* off it! [*He twists her wrist.*] Ouuuu! Stop it, stop it, stop it!

JAKE: Where have I been since supper?

FLORA: Here, here! On th' porch! Fo' God's sake, quit that twistin'!

JAKE: Where have I been?

FLORA: Porch! Porch! Here!

JAKE: Doin' what?

FLORA: *Jake!*

JAKE: Doin' what?

FLORA: Lemme go! Christ, Jake! Let loose! Quit twisting, you'll break my wrist!

JAKE [*laughing between his teeth*]: Doin' what? What doin'? Since supper?

FLORA [*crying out*]: How in hell do I know!

JAKE: 'Cause you was right here with me, all the time, for every second! You an' me, sweetheart, was sittin' here together on th' swing, just swingin' back an' forth every minute since supper! You got that in your haid good now?

7

FLORA [*whimpering*]: Le' go!

JAKE: Got it? In your haid good now?

FLORA: Yeh, yeh, yeh—leggo!

JAKE: What was I doin', then?

FLORA: Swinging! For Christ's sake—swingin'! [*He releases her. She whimpers and rubs her wrist but the impression is that the experience was not without pleasure for both parties. She groans and whimpers. He grips her loose curls in his hand and bends her head back. He plants a long wet kiss on her mouth.*]

FLORA [*whimpering*]: Mmmm-hmmmm! Mmmm! Mmmm!

JAKE [*huskily*]: Tha's my swee' baby girl.

FLORA: Mmmmm! Hurt! Hurt!

JAKE: Hurt?

FLORA: Mmmm! Hurt!

JAKE: Kiss?

FLORA: Mmmm!

JAKE: Good?

FLORA: Mmmm . . .

JAKE: Good! Make little room.

FLORA: Too hot!

JAKE: Go on, make little room.

FLORA: Mmmmm . . .

JAKE: Crosspatch?

FLORA: Mmmmmm.

JAKE: Whose baby? Big? Sweet?

FLORA: Mmmmm! Hurt!

JAKE: Kiss! [*He lifts her wrist to his lips and makes gobbling sounds.*]

FLORA [*giggling*]: Stop! Silly! Mmmm!

JAKE: What would I do if you was a big piece of cake?

FLORA: Silly.

JAKE: Gobble! Gobble!

FLORA: Oh, you—

JAKE: What would I do if you was angel food cake? Big white piece with lots of nice thick icin'?

FLORA [*giggling*]: Quit!

JAKE: Gobble, gobble, gobble!

FLORA [*squealing*]: Jake!

JAKE: Huh?

FLORA: You *tick*-le!

JAKE: Answer little question!

FLORA: Wh-at?

JAKE: Where I been since supper?

FLORA: Off in the Chevy! [*He instantly seizes the wrist again. She shrieks.*]

JAKE: Where've I been since supper?

FLORA: Po'ch! Swing!

JAKE: Doin' what?

FLORA: *Swingin'!* Oh, Christ, Jake, let loose!

JAKE: Hurt?

FLORA: Mmmmm . . .

JAKE: Good?

FLORA [*whimpering*]: Mmmmm . . .

JAKE: Now you know where I been an' what I been doin' since supper?

FLORA: Yeah . . .

JAKE: Case anybody should ask?

FLORA: Who's going to ast?

10

JAKE: Never mind who's goin' t' ast, just you know the answers! Uh-huh?

FLORA: Uh-huh [*lisping babyishly*]. This is where you been. Settin' on th' swing since we had supper. Swingin'—back an' fo'th—back an' fo'th. . . . You didn' go off in th' Chevy [*slowly*] an' you was awf'ly surprised w'en th' Syndicate fire broke out! [*Jake slaps her.*] Jake!

JAKE: Everything you said is awright. But don't you get ideas.

FLORA: Ideas?

JAKE: A woman like you's not made to have ideas. Made to be hugged an' squeezed!

FLORA [*babyishly*]: Mmmm. . . .

JAKE: But not for ideas. So don't you have ideas. [*He rises.*] Go out an' get in th' Chevy.

FLORA: We goin to th' fire?

JAKE: No. We ain' goin' no fire. We goin' in town an' get us a case a dopes because we're hot an' thirsty.

FLORA [*vaguely, as she rises*]: I lost m' white—kid—purse . . .

JAKE: It's on the seat of th' Chevy whe' you left it.

FLORA: Whe' *you* goin'?

JAKE: I'm goin in t' th' toilet. I'll be right out. [*He goes inside, letting the screen door slam. Flora shuffles to the edge of the steps and stands there with a slight idiotic smile. She begins to descend, letting herself down each time with the same foot,*

11

like a child just learning to walk. She stops at the bottom of the steps and stares at the sky, vacantly and raptly, her fingers closing gently around the bruised wrist. Jake can be heard singing inside.]

My baby don' care fo' rings
or other expensive things—
My baby just cares—fo'—me!

CURTAIN

It is just after noon. The sky is the color of the satin bows on the window curtains—a translucent, innocent blue. Heat devils are shimmering over the flat Delta country and the peaked white front of the house is like a shrill exclamation. Jake's gin is busy, heard like a steady pulse across the road. A delicate lint of cotton is drifting about in the atmosphere.

Jake appears, a large and purposeful man with arms like hams covered with a fuzz of fine blond hair. He is followed by Silva Vicarro who is the Superintendent of the Syndicate Plantation where the fire occurred last night. Vicarro is a rather small and wiry man of dark Latin looks and nature. He wears whipcord breeches, laced boots, and a white undershirt. He has a Roman Catholic medallion on a chain about his neck.

JAKE [*with the good-natured condescension of a very large man for a small one*]: Well, suh, all I got to say is you're a mighty lucky little fellow.

VICARRO: Lucky? In what way?

JAKE: That I can take on a job like this right now! Twenty-seven wagons full of cotton 's a pretty big piece of bus'ness, Mr. Vicarro. [*Stopping at the steps*] Baby! [*He bites off a piece of tobacco plug.*] What's yuh firs' name?

VICARRO: Silva.

JAKE: How do you spell it?

VICARRO: S-I-L-V-A.

JAKE: Silva! Like a silver lining! Ev'ry cloud has got a silver lining. What does that come from? The Bible?

13

VICARRO [*sitting on the steps*]: No. The Mother Goose Book.

JAKE: Well, suh, you sure are lucky that I can do it. If I'd been busy like I was two weeks ago, I would 've turned it down. *BABY! COME OUT HERE A MINUTE!* [*There is a vague response from inside.*]

VICARRO: Lucky, Very lucky. [*He lights a cigarette. Flora pushes open the screen door and comes out. She has on her watermelon pink silk dress and is clutching against her body the big white kid purse with her initials on it in big nickel plate.*]

JAKE [*proudly*]: Mr. Vicarro—I want you to meet Mrs. Meighan. Baby, this is a very down-at-the-mouth young fellow I want you to cheer up fo' me. He thinks he's out of luck because his cotton gin burnt down. He's got twenty-seven wagons full of cotton to be ginned out on a hurry-up order from his most impo'tant customers in Mobile. Well, suh, I said to him, Mr. Vicarro, you're to be congratulated—not because it burnt down, but because I happen to be in a situation to take the business over. Now you tell him just how lucky he is!

FLORA [*nervously*]: Well, I guess he don't see how it was lucky to have his gin burned down.

VICARRO [*acidly*]: No, ma'am.

JAKE [*quickly*]: Mr. Vicarro. Some fellows marry a girl when she's little an' tiny. They like a small figure. See? Then, when the girl gets comfo'tably settled down—what does she do? Puts on flesh—of cou'se!

FLORA [*bashfully*]: Jake!

JAKE: Now then! How do they react? Accept it as a matter of cou'se, as something which 'as been ordained by nature?

14

Nope! No, suh, not a bit! They sta't to feeling abused. They think that fate must have a grudge against them because the little woman is not so little as she used to be. Because she's gone an' put on a matronly figure. Well, suh, that's at the root of a lot of domestic trouble. However, Mr. Vicarro, I never made that mistake. When I fell in love with this baby-doll I've got here, she was just the same size then that you see her today.

FLORA [*crossing shyly to porch rail*]: Jake . . .

JAKE [*grinning*]: A woman not large but tremendous! That's how I liked her—tremendous! I told her right off, when I slipped th' ring on her finger, one Satiddy night in a boathouse on Moon Lake—I said to her, Honey, if you take off one single pound of that body—I'm going to quit yuh! I'm going to quit yuh, I said, the minute I notice you've started to take off weight!

FLORA: Aw, Jake—please!

JAKE: I don't want nothing little, not in a woman. I'm not after nothing *petite,* as the Frenchmen call it. This is what I wanted—and what I *got!* Look at her, Mr. Vicarro. Look at her blush! [*He grips the back of Flora's neck and tries to turn her around.*]

FLORA: Aw, quit, Jake! Quit, will yuh?

JAKE: See what a doll she is? [*Flora turns suddenly and spanks him with the kid purse. He cackles and runs down the steps. At the corner of the house, he stops and turns.*] Baby, you keep Mr. Vicarro comfo'table while I'm ginnin' out that twenty-seven wagons full of cotton. Th' good-neighbor policy, Mr. Vicarro. You do me a good turn an' I'll do you a good one! Be see'n' yuh! So long, Baby! [*He walks away with an energetic stride.*]

15

VICARRO: The good-neighbor policy! [*He sits on the porch steps.*]

FLORA [*sitting on the swing*]: Izzen he out-*ray*-juss! [*She laughs foolishly and puts the purse in her lap. Vicarro stares gloomily across the dancing brilliance of the fields. His lip sticks out like a pouting child's. A rooster crows in the distance.*]

FLORA: I would'n' dare to expose myself like that.

VICARRO: Expose? To what?

FLORA: The sun. I take a terrible burn. I'll never forget the burn I took one time. It was on Moon Lake one Sunday before I was married. I never did like t' go fishin' but this young fellow, one of the Peterson boys, insisted that we go fishin'. Well, he didn't catch nothin' but jus' kep' fishin' an' fishin' an' I set there in th' boat with all that hot sun on me. I said, Stay under the willows. But he would'n' lissen to me, an' sure enough I took such an awful burn I had t' sleep on m' stummick th' nex' three nights.

VICARRO [*absently*]: What did you say? You got sunburned?

FLORA: Yes. One time on Moon Lake.

VICARRO: That's too bad. You got over it all right?

FLORA: Oh, yes. Finally. Yes.

VICARRO: That must 've been pretty bad.

FLORA: I fell in the lake once, too. Also with one of the Peterson boys. On another fishing trip. That was a wild bunch of boys, those Peterson boys. I never went out with 'em but something happened which made me wish I hadn't. One time, sun-

16

burned. One time, nearly drowned. One time—poison ivy! Well, lookin' back on it, now, we had a good deal of fun in spite of it, though.

VICARRO: The good-neighbor policy, huh? [*He slaps his boot with the riding crop. Then he rises from steps.*]

FLORA: You might as well come up on th' po'ch an' make you'self as comfo'table as you can.

VICARRO: Uh-huh.

FLORA: I'm not much good at—makin' conversation.

VICARRO [*finally noticing her*]: Now don't you bother to make conversation for my benefit, Mrs. Meighan. I'm the type that prefers a quiet understanding. [*Flora laughs uncertainly.*] One thing I always notice about you ladies . . .

FLORA: What's that, Mr. Vicarro?

VICARRO: You always have something in your hands—to hold onto. Now that kid purse . . .

FLORA: My purse?

VICARRO: You have no reason to keep that purse in your hands. You're certainly not afraid that I'm going to snatch it!

FLORA: Oh, God, no! I wassen afraid of that!

VICARRO: That wouldn't be the good-neighbor policy, would it? But you hold onto that purse because it gives you something to get a grip on. Isn't that right?

FLORA: Yes. I always like to have something in my hands.

17

VICARRO: Sure you do. You feel what a lot of uncertain things there are. Gins burn down. The volunteer fire department don't have decent equipment. Nothing is any protection. The afternoon sun is hot. It's no protection. The trees are back of the house. They're no protection. The goods that dress is made of— is no protection. So what do you do, Mrs. Meighan? You pick up the white kid purse. It's solid. It's sure. It's certain. It's something to hold *on* to. You get what I mean?

FLORA: Yeah. I think I do.

VICARRO: It gives you a feeling of being attached to something. The mother protects the baby? No, no, no—the baby protects the mother! From being lost and empty and having nothing but lifeless things in her hands! Maybe you think there isn't much connection!

FLORA: You'll have to excuse me from thinking. I'm too lazy.

VICARRO: What's your name, Mrs. Meighan?

FLORA: Flora.

VICARRO: Mine is Silva. Something not gold but—Silva!

FLORA: Like a silver dollar?

VICARRO: No, like a silver dime! It's an Italian name. I'm a native of New Orleans.

FLORA: Then it's not sunburn. You're natcherally dark.

VICARRO [*raising his undershirt from his belly*]: Look at this!

FLORA: Mr. Vicarro!

VICARRO: Just as dark as my arm is!

FLORA: You don't have to show me! I'm not from Missouri!

VICARRO [*grinning*]: Excuse me.

FLORA [*laughing nervously*]: Whew! I'm sorry to say we don't have a Coke in the house. We meant to get a case of Cokes las' night, but what with all the excitement going on—

VICARRO: What excitement was that?

FLORA: Oh, the fire and all.

VICARRO [*lighting a cigarette*]: I shouldn't think you all would of been excited about the fire.

FLORA: A fire is always exciting. After a fire, dogs an' chickens don't sleep. I don't think our chickens got to sleep all night.

VICARRO: No?

FLORA: They cackled an' fussed an' flopped around on the roost—took on something awful! Myself, I couldn't sleep neither. I jus' lay there an' sweated all night long.

VICARRO: On account of th' fire?

FLORA: An' the heat an' mosquitoes. And I was mad at Jake.

VICARRO: Mad at Mr. Meighan? What about?

FLORA: Oh, he went off an' left me settin' here on this ole po'ch last night without a Coca-Cola on the place.

VICARRO: Went off an' left you, did he?

FLORA: Yep. Right after supper. An' when he got back the fire 'd already broke out an' instead of drivin' into town like he said, he decided to go an' take a look at your burnt-down cotton gin. I got smoke in my eyes an' my nose an' throat. It hurt my sinus an' I was in such a wo'n-out, nervous condition, it made me cry. I cried like a baby. Finally took two teaspoons of paregoric. Enough to put an elephant to sleep. But still I stayed awake an' heard them chickens carryin' on out there!

VICARRO: It sounds like you passed a very uncomfortable night.

FLORA: Sounds like? Well, it *was*.

VICARRO: So Mr. Meighan—you say—disappeared after supper? [*There is a pause while Flora looks at him blankly.*]

FLORA: Huh?

VICARRO: You say Mr. Meighan was out of the house for a while after supper? [*Something in his tone makes her aware of her indiscretion.*]

FLORA: Oh—uh—just for a moment.

VICARRO: Just for a moment, huh? How long a moment? [*He stares at her very hard.*]

FLORA: What are you driving at, Mr. Vicarro?

VICARRO: Driving at? Nothing.

FLORA: You're looking at me so funny.

VICARRO: He disappeared for a moment! Is that what he did? How long a moment did he disappear for? Can you remember, Mrs. Meighan?

FLORA: What difference does that make? What's it to you, anyhow?

VICARRO: Why should you mind me asking!

FLORA: You make this sound like I was on trial for something!

VICARRO: Don't you like to pretend like you're a witness?

FLORA: Witness of what, Mr. Vicarro?

VICARRO: Why—for instance—say—a case of arson!

FLORA [*wetting her lips*]: Case of—? What is—arson?

VICARRO: The willful destruction of property by fire. [*He slaps his boots sharply with the riding crop.*]

FLORA [*startled*]: Oh! [*She nervously fingers the purse.*] Well, now, don't you go and be getting any—funny ideas.

VICARRO: Ideas about what, Mrs. Meighan?

FLORA: My husband's disappearin'—after supper. I can explain that.

VICARRO: Can you?

FLORA: Sure I can.

VICARRO: Good! How do you explain it? [*He stares at her. She looks down.*] What's the matter? Can't you collect your thoughts, Mrs. Meighan?

FLORA: No, but—

21

VICARRO: Your mind's a blank on the subject?

FLORA: Look here, now— [*She squirms on the swing.*]

VICARRO: You find it impossible to remember just what your husband disappeared for after supper? You can't imagine what kind of errand it was that he went out on, can you?

FLORA: No! No, I can't!

VICARRO: But when he returned—let's see . . . The fire had just broken out at the Syndicate Plantation?

FLORA: Mr. Vicarro, I don't have the slightest idear what you could be driving at.

VICARRO: You're a very unsatisfactory witness, Mrs. Meighan.

FLORA: I never can think when people—stare straight at me.

VICARRO: Okay. I'll look away, then. [*He turns his back to her.*] Now does that improve your memory any? Now are you able to concentrate on the question?

FLORA: Huh . . .

VICARRO: No? You're not? [*He turns around again, grinning evilly.*] Well . . . shall we drop the subject?

FLORA: I sure do wish you would.

VICARRO: It's no use crying over a burnt-down gin. This world is built on the principle of tit for tat.

FLORA: What do you mean?

VICARRO: Nothing at all specific. Mind if I . . . ?

FLORA: What?

VICARRO: You want to move over a little an' make some room? [*Flora edges aside on the swing. He sits down with her.*] I like a swing. I've always liked to sit an' rock on a swing. Relaxes you. . . . You relaxed?

FLORA: Sure.

VICARRO: No, you're not. Your nerves are all tied up.

FLORA: Well, you made me feel kind of nervous. All of them questions you ast me about the fire.

VICARRO: I didn' ask you questions about the fire. I only asked you about your husband's leaving the house after supper.

FLORA: I explained that to you.

VICARRO: Sure. That's right. You did. The good-neighbor policy. That was a lovely remark your husband made about the good-neighbor policy. I see what he means by that now.

FLORA: He was thinking about President Roosevelt's speech. We sat up an' lissened to it one night last week.

VICARRO: No, I think that he was talking about something closer to home, Mrs. Meighan. You do me a good turn and I'll do you one, that was the way that he put it. You have a piece of cotton on your face. Hold still—I'll pick it off. [*He delicately removes the lint.*] There now.

FLORA [*nervously*]: Thanks.

23

VICARRO: There's a lot of fine cotton lint floating round in the air.

FLORA: I know there is. It irritates my nose. I think it gets up in my sinus.

VICARRO: Well, you're a delicate woman.

FLORA: Delicate? Me? Oh, no. I'm too big for that.

VICARRO: Your size is part of your delicacy, Mrs. Meighan.

FLORA: How do you mean?

VICARRO: There's a lot of you, but every bit of you is delicate. Choice. Delectable, I might say.

FLORA: Huh?

VICARRO: I mean you're altogether lacking in any—coarseness. You're soft. Fine-fibered. And smooth.

FLORA: Our talk is certainly taking a personal turn.

VICARRO: Yes. You make me think of cotton.

FLORA: Huh?

VICARRO: Cotton!

FLORA: Well! Should I say thanks or something?

VICARRO: No, just smile, Mrs. Meighan. You have an attractive smile. Dimples!

FLORA: No . . .

VICARRO: Yes, you have! Smile, Mrs. Meighan! Come on—smile! [*Flora averts her face, smiling helplessly.*] There now. See? You've got them! [*He delicately touches one of the dimples.*]

FLORA: Please don't touch me. I don't like to be touched.

VICARRO: Then why do you giggle?

FLORA: Can't help it. You make me feel kind of hysterical, Mr. Vicarro. Mr. Vicarro—

VICARRO: Yes?

FLORA: I hope you don't think that Jake was mixed up in that fire. I swear to goodness he never left the front porch. I remember it perfeckly now. We just set here on the swing till the fire broke out and then we drove in town.

VICARRO: To celebrate?

FLORA: No, no, no.

VICARRO: Twenty-seven wagons full of cotton's a pretty big piece of business to fall in your lap like a gift from the gods, Mrs. Meighan.

FLORA: I thought you said that we would drop the subjeck.

VICARRO: You brought it up that time.

FLORA: Well, please don't try to mix me up any more. I swear to goodness the fire had already broke out when he got back.

VICARRO: That's not what you told me a moment ago.

FLORA: You got me all twisted up. We went in town. The fire broke out an' we didn't know about it.

25

VICARRO: I thought you said it irritated your sinus.

FLORA: Oh, my God, you sure put words in my mouth. Maybe I'd better make us some lemonade.

VICARRO: Don't go to the trouble.

FLORA: I'll go in an' fix it direckly, but right at this moment I'm too weak to get up. I don't know why, but I can't hardly hold my eyes open. They keep falling shut. . . . I think it's a little too crowded, two on a swing. Will you do me a favor an' set back down over there?

VICARRO: Why do you want me to move?

FLORA: It makes too much body heat when we're crowded together.

VICARRO: One body can borrow coolness from another.

FLORA: I always heard that bodies borrowed heat.

VICARRO: Not in this case. I'm cool.

FLORA: You don't seem like it to me.

VICARRO: I'm just as cool as a cucumber. If you don't believe it, touch me.

FLORA: Where?

VICARRO: Anywhere.

FLORA [rising with great effort]: Excuse me. I got to go in. [He pulls her back down.] What did you do that for?

VICARRO: I don't want to be deprived of your company yet.

26

FLORA: Mr. Vicarro, you're getting awf'ly familiar.

VICARRO: Haven't you got any fun-loving spirit about you?

FLORA: This isn't fun.

VICARRO: Then why do you giggle?

FLORA: I'm ticklish! Quit switching me, will yuh?

VICARRO: I'm just shooing the flies off.

FLORA: Leave 'em be, then, please. They don't hurt nothin'.

VICARRO: I think you like to be switched.

FLORA: I don't. I wish you'd quit.

VICARRO: You'd like to be switched harder.

FLORA: No, I wouldn't.

VICARRO: That blue mark on your wrist—

FLORA: What about it?

VICARRO: I've got a suspicion.

FLORA: Of what?

VICARRO: It was twisted. By your husband.

FLORA: You're crazy.

VICARRO: Yes, it was. And you liked it.

FLORA: I certainly didn't. Would you mind moving your arm?

27

VICARRO: Don't be so skittish.

FLORA: Awright. I'll get up then.

VICARRO: Go on.

FLORA: I feel so weak.

VICARRO: Dizzy?

FLORA: A little bit. Yeah. My head's spinning round. I wish you would stop the swing.

VICARRO: It's not swinging much.

FLORA: But even a little's too much.

VICARRO: You're a delicate woman. A pretty big woman, too.

FLORA: So is America. Big.

VICARRO: That's a funny remark.

FLORA: Yeah. I don't know why I made it. My head's so buzzy.

VICARRO: Fuzzy?

FLORA: Fuzzy an'—buzzy. . . . Is something on my arm?

VICARRO: No.

FLORA: Then what 're you brushing?

VICARRO: Sweat off.

FLORA: Leave it alone.

VICARRO: Let me wipe it. [*He brushes her arm with a handker-chief.*]

FLORA [*laughing weakly*]: No, please, don't. It feels funny.

VICARRO: How does it feel?

FLORA: It tickles me. All up an' down. You cut it out now. If you don't cut it out I'm going to call.

VICARRO: Call who?

FLORA: I'm going to call that nigger. The nigger that's cutting the grass across the road.

VICARRO: Go on. Call, then.

FLORA [*weakly*]: Hey! Hey, boy!

VICARRO: Can't you call any louder?

FLORA: I feel so funny. What is the matter with me?

VICARRO: You're just relaxing. You're big. A big type of woman. I like you. Don't get so excited.

FLORA: I'm not, but you—

VICARRO: What am I doing?

FLORA: Suspicions. About my husband and ideas you have about me.

VICARRO: Such as what?

FLORA: He burnt your gin down. He didn't. And I'm not a big piece of cotton. [*She pulls herself up.*] I'm going inside.

VICARRO [*rising*]: I think that's a good idea.

FLORA: I said I was. Not you.

VICARRO: Why not me?

FLORA: Inside it might be crowded, with you an' me.

VICARRO: Three's a crowd. We're two.

FLORA: You stay out. Wait here.

VICARRO: What'll you do?

FLORA: I'll make us a pitcher of nice cold lemonade.

VICARRO: Okay. You go on in.

FLORA: What'll you do?

VICARRO: I'll follow.

FLORA: That's what I figured you might be aiming to do. We'll both stay out.

VICARRO: In the sun?

FLORA: We'll sit back down in th' shade. [*He blocks her.*] Don't stand in my way.

VICARRO: You're standing in mine.

FLORA: I'm dizzy.

VICARRO: You ought to lie down.

FLORA: How can I?

VICARRO: Go in.

FLORA: You'd follow me.

VICARRO: What if I did?

FLORA: I'm afraid.

VICARRO: You're starting to cry.

FLORA: I'm afraid!

VICARRO: What of?

FLORA: Of you.

VICARRO: I'm little.

FLORA: I'm dizzy. My knees are so weak they're like water. I've got to sit down.

VICARRO: Go in.

FLORA: I can't.

VICARRO: Why not?

FLORA: You'd follow.

VICARRO: Would that be so awful?

FLORA: You've got a mean look in your eyes and I don't like the whip. Honest to God he never. He didn't, I swear!

VICARRO: Do what?

FLORA: The fire . . .

31

VICARRO: Go on.

FLORA: Please don't!

VICARRO: Don't what?

FLORA: Put it down. The whip, please put it down. Leave it out here on the porch.

VICARRO: What are you scared of?

FLORA: You.

VICARRO: Go on. [*She turns helplessly and moves to the screen. He pulls it open.*]

FLORA: Don't follow. Please don't follow! [*She sways uncertainly. He presses his hand against her. She moves inside. He follows. The door is shut quietly. The gin pumps slowly and steadily across the road. From inside the house there is a wild and despairing cry. A door is slammed. The cry is repeated more faintly.*]

CURTAIN

*It is about nine o'clock the same evening. Although the sky be-
hind the house is a dusky rose color, a full September moon of
almost garish intensity gives the front of the house a ghostly
brilliance. Dogs are howling like demons across the prostrate
fields of the Delta.*

The front porch of the Meighans is empty.

*After a moment the screen door is pushed slowly open and
Flora Meighan emerges gradually. Her appearance is ravaged.
Her eyes have a vacant limpidity in the moonlight, her lips are
slightly apart. She moves with her hands stretched gropingly
before her till she has reached a pillar of the porch. There she
stops and stands moaning a little. Her hair hangs loose and dis-
ordered. The upper part of her body is unclothed except for a
torn pink band about her breasts. Dark streaks are visible on the
bare shoulders and arms and there is a large discoloration along
one cheek. A dark trickle, now congealed, descends from one
corner of her mouth. These more apparent tokens she covers
with one hand when Jake comes up on the porch. He is now
heard approaching, singing to himself.*

JAKE: By the light—by the light—by the light—Of the sil-very
mo-o-on! [*Instinctively Flora draws back into the sharply
etched shadow from the porch roof. Jake is too tired and triumphant to notice her appearance.*] How's a baby? [*Flora utters a
moaning grunt.*] Tired? Too tired t' talk? Well, that's how I
feel. Too tired t' talk. Too goddam tired t' speak a friggin'
word! [*He lets himself down on the steps, groaning and without giving Flora more than a glance.*] Twenty-seven wagons
full of cotton. That's how much I've ginned since ten this
mawnin'. A man-size job.

FLORA [*huskily*]: Uh-huh. . . . A man-size—job. . . .

JAKE: *Twen*-ty *sev*-en *wa*-gons *full* of *cot*-ton!

FLORA [*senselessly repeating*]: *Twen*-ty *sev*-en *wa*-gons *full* of *cot*-ton! [*A dog howls. Flora utters a breathless laugh.*]

JAKE: What're you laughin' at, honey? Not at me, I hope.

FLORA: No. . . .

JAKE: That's good. The job that I've turned out is nothing to laugh at. I drove that pack of niggers like a mule skinner. They don't have a brain in their bodies. All they got is bodies. You got to drive, drive, drive. I don't even see how niggers eat without somebody to tell them to put the food in their moufs! [*She laughs again, like water spilling out of her mouth.*] Huh! You got a laugh like a— Christ. A terrific day's work I finished.

FLORA [*slowly*]: I would'n' brag—about it. . . .

JAKE: I'm not braggin' about it, I'm just sayin' I done a big day's work, I'm all wo'n out an' I want a little appreciation, not cross speeches. Honey. . . .

FLORA: I'm not—[*She laughs again.*]—makin' cross speeches.

JAKE: To take on a big piece of work an' finish it up an' mention the fack that it's finished I wouldn't call braggin'.

FLORA: You're not the only one's—done a big day's—work.

JAKE: Who else that you know of? [*There is a pause.*]

FLORA: Maybe you think that I had an easy time. [*Her laughter spills out again.*]

JAKE: You're laughin' like you been on a goddam jag. [*Flora laughs.*] What did you get pissed on? Roach poison or citronella? I think I make it pretty easy for you, workin' like a mule

34

skinner so you can hire you a nigger to do the wash an' take the housework on. An elephant woman who acks as frail as a kitten, that's the kind of a woman I got on m' hands.

FLORA: Sure. ·. . . [*She laughs.*] You make it easy!

JAKE: I've yet t' see you lift a little finger. Even gotten too lazy t' put you' things on. Round the house ha'f naked all th' time. Y' live in a cloud. All you can think of is "Give me a Coca-Cola!" Well, you better look out. They got a new bureau in the guvamint files. It's called U.W. Stands for Useless Wimmen. Tha's secret plans on foot t' have 'em shot! [*He laughs at his joke.*]

FLORA: Secret—plans—on foot?

JAKE: T' have 'em *shot.*

FLORA: That's good. I'm glad t' hear it. [*She laughs again.*]

JAKE: I come home tired an' you cain't wait t' peck at me. What 're you cross about now?

FLORA: I think it was a mistake.

JAKE: What was a mistake?

FLORA: Fo' you t' fool with th' Syndicate—Plantation. . . .

JAKE: I don't know about that. We wuh kind of up against it, honey. Th' Syndicate buyin' up all th' lan' aroun' here an' turnin' the ole croppers off it without their wages—mighty near busted ev'ry mercantile store in Two Rivers County! An' then they build their own gin to gin their own cotton. It looked for a while like I was stuck up high an' dry. But when the gin burnt down an' Mr. Vicarro decided he'd better throw a little bus'ness my way—I'd say the situation was much improved!

FLORA [*laughing weakly*]: Then maybe you don't understand th' good-neighbor—policy.

JAKE: Don't understand it? Why, I'm the boy that invented it.

FLORA: Huh-huh! What an—*invention!* All I can say is—I hope you're satisfied now that you've ginned out—twenty-seven wagons full of—cotton.

JAKE: Vicarro was pretty well pleased w'en he dropped over.

FLORA: Yeah. He was—pretty well—pleased.

JAKE: How did you all get along?

FLORA: We got along jus' fine. Jus' fine an'—dandy.

JAKE: He didn't seem like a such a bad little guy. He takes a sensible attitude.

FLORA [*laughing helplessly*]: He—sure—does!

JAKE: I hope you made him comfo'table in the house?

FLORA [*giggling*]: I made him a pitcher—of nice cold—lemonade!

JAKE: With a little gin in it, huh? That's how you got pissed. A nice cool drink don't sound bad to me right now. Got any left?

FLORA: Not a bit, Mr. Meighan. We drank it *a-a-ll* up! [*She flops onto the swing.*]

JAKE: So you didn't have such a tiresome time after all?

NEGRO [*solemnly nodding*]: The graveyard is crowded with folks we knew, Mistuh Charlie. It's mighty late in the day!

MR. CHARLIE: Huh! [*He crosses to the window.*] Nigguh, it ain't even late in the day any more— [*He throws up the blind.*] It's NIGHT! [*The space of the window is black.*]

NEGRO [*softly, with a wise old smile*]: Yes, suh . . . *Night,* Mistuh Charlie!

CURTAIN

PORTRAIT OF A MADONNA

IIIIIIIIIIIIIIIIIIIIIIIIIIIIIIIIIIIIIIIIIIIIIIIIIIIIIIIIIIIIIIIIIIIIIIIIIIIIIIIIIIIIIIIIIIIIIIIIIIIIIIIIIIIIIIIIIIIIIIIIIIIIIIIIIIIIIIIIIIIIIIIIIIIIIIIIIII

RESPECTFULLY DEDICATED TO THE TALENT
AND CHARM OF MISS LILLIAN GISH.

CHARACTERS

MISS LUCRETIA COLLINS

THE PORTER

THE ELEVATOR BOY

THE DOCTOR

THE NURSE

MR. ABRAMS

PORTRAIT OF A MADONNA

The living room of a moderate-priced city apartment. The furnishings are old-fashioned and everything is in a state of neglect and disorder. There is a door in the back wall to a bedroom, and on the right to the outside hall.

MISS COLLINS: Richard! [*The door bursts open and Miss Collins rushes out, distractedly. She is a middle-aged spinster, very slight and hunched of figure with a desiccated face that is flushed with excitement. Her hair is arranged in curls that would become a young girl and she wears a frilly negligee which might have come from an old hope chest of a period considerably earlier.*] No, no, no, no! I don't care if the whole church hears about it! [*She frenziedly snatches up the phone.*] Manager, I've got to speak to the manager! Hurry, oh, please hurry, there's a *man*—! [*wildly aside as if to an invisible figure*] Lost all respect, absolutely no respect! . . . Mr. Abrams? [*in a tense hushed voice*] I don't want any reporters to hear about this but something awful has been going on upstairs. Yes, this is Miss Collins' apartment on the top floor. I've refrained from making any complaint because of my connections with the church. I used to be assistant to the Sunday School superintendent and I once had the primary class. I helped them put on the Christmas pageant. I made the dress for the Virgin and Mòther, made robes for the Wise Men. Yes, and now this has happened, I'm not responsible for it, but night after night after night this man has been coming into my apartment and—indulging his senses! Do you understand? Not once but repeatedly, Mr. Abrams! I don't know whether he comes in the door or the window or up the fire escape or whether there's some secret entrance they know about at the church, but he's here now, in my bedroom, and I can't force him to leave, I'll have to have some assistance! No, he isn't a thief, Mr. Abrams, he comes of a very fine family in Webb, Mississippi, but this woman has ruined his character, she's destroyed his respect for ladies! Mr. Abrams? Mr.

Abrams! Oh, goodness! [*She slams up the receiver and looks distractedly about for a moment; then rushes back into the bedroom.*] Richard! [*The door slams shut. After a few moments an old porter enters in drab gray coveralls. He looks about with a sorrowfully humorous curiosity, then timidly calls.*]

PORTER: Miss Collins? [*The elevator door slams open in hall and the Elevator Boy, wearing a uniform, comes in.*]

ELEVATOR BOY: Where is she?

PORTER: Gone in 'er bedroom.

ELEVATOR BOY [*grinning*]: She got him in there with her?

PORTER: Sounds like it. [*Miss Collins' voice can be heard faintly protesting with the mysterious intruder.*]

ELEVATOR BOY: What'd Abrams tell yuh to do?

PORTER: Stay here an' keep a watch on 'er till they git here.

ELEVATOR BOY: Jesus.

PORTER: Close 'at door.

ELEVATOR BOY: I gotta leave it open a little so I can hear the buzzer. Ain't this place a holy sight though?

PORTER: Don't look like it's had a good cleaning in fifteen or twenty years. I bet it ain't either. Abrams'll bust a blood vessel when he takes a lookit them walls.

ELEVATOR BOY: How comes it's in this condition?

PORTER: She wouldn't let no one in.

ELEVATOR BOY: Not even the paperhangers?

PORTER: Naw. Not even the plumbers. The plaster washed down in the bathroom underneath hers an' she admitted her plumbin' had been stopped up. Mr. Abrams had to let the plumber in with this here passkey when she went out for a while.

ELEVATOR BOY: Holy Jeez. I wunner if she's got money stashed around here. A lotta freaks do stick away big sums of money in ole mattresses an' things.

PORTER: She ain't. She got a monthly pension check or something she always turned over to Mr. Abrams to dole it out to 'er. She tole him that Southern ladies was never brought up to manage finanshul affairs. Lately the checks quit comin'.

ELEVATOR BOY: Yeah?

PORTER: The pension give out or somethin'. Abrams says he got a contribution from the church to keep 'er on here without 'er knowin' about it. She's proud as a peacock's tail in spite of 'er awful appearance.

ELEVATOR BOY: Lissen to 'er in there!

PORTER: What's she sayin'?

ELEVATOR BOY: Apologizin' to him! For callin' the *police!*

PORTER: She thinks police 're comin'?

MISS COLLINS [*from bedroom*]: Stop it, it's got to stop!

ELEVATOR BOY: Fightin' to protect her honor again! What a commotion, no wunner folks are complainin'!

111

PORTER [*lighting his pipe*]: This here'll be the last time.

ELEVATOR BOY: She's goin' out, huh?

PORTER [*blowing out the match*]: Tonight.

ELEVATOR BOY: Where'll she go?

PORTER [*slowly moving to the old gramophone*]: She'll go to the state asylum.

ELEVATOR BOY: Holy G!

PORTER: Remember this ole number? [*He puts on a record of "I'm Forever Blowing Bubbles."*]

ELEVATOR BOY: Naw. When did that come out?

PORTER: Before your time, sonny boy. Machine needs oilin'.

[*He takes out small oil-can and applies oil about the crank and other parts of gramophone.*]

ELEVATOR BOY: How long is the old girl been here?

PORTER: Abrams says she's been livin' here twenty-five, thirty years, since before he got to be manager even.

ELEVATOR BOY: Livin' alone all that time?

PORTER: She had an old mother died of an operation about fifteen years ago. Since then she ain't gone out of the place excep' on Sundays to church or Friday nights to some kind of religious meeting.

ELEVATOR BOY: Got an awful lot of ol' magazines piled aroun' here.

PORTER: She used to collect 'em. She'd go out in back and fish 'em out of the incinerator.

ELEVATOR BOY: What'n hell for?

PORTER: Mr. Abrams says she used to cut out the Campbell soup kids. Them red-tomato-headed kewpie dolls that go with the soup advertisements. You seen 'em, ain'tcha?

ELEVATOR BOY: Uh-huh.

PORTER: She made a collection of 'em. Filled a big lot of scrapbooks with them paper kiddies an' took 'em down to the Children's Hospitals on Xmas Eve an' Easter Sunday, exactly twicet a year. Sounds better, don't it? [*referring to gramophone, which resumes its faint, wheedling music*] Eliminated some a that crankin' noise . . .

ELEVATOR BOY: I didn't know that she'd been nuts *that* long.

PORTER: Who's nuts an' who ain't? If you ask me the world is populated with people that's just as peculiar as she is.

ELEVATOR BOY: Hell. She don't have brain *one*.

PORTER: There's important people in Europe got less'n she's got. Tonight they're takin' her off 'n' lockin' her up. They'd do a lot better to leave 'er go an' lock up some a them maniacs over there. She's harmless; they ain't. They kill millions of people an' go scot free!

ELEVATOR BOY: An ole woman like her is disgusting, though, imaginin' somebody's raped her.

113

PORTER: Pitiful, not disgusting. Watch out for them cigarette ashes.

ELEVATOR BOY: What's uh diff'rence? So much dust you can't see it. All a this here goes out in the morning, don't it?

PORTER: Uh-huh.

ELEVATOR BOY: I think I'll take a couple a those ole records as curiosities for my girl friend. She's got a portable in 'er bedroom, she says it's better with music!

PORTER: Leave 'em alone. She's still got 'er property rights.

ELEVATOR BOY: Aw, she's got all she wants with them dream-lovers of hers!

PORTER: *Hush up!* [*He makes a warning gesture as Miss Collins enters from bedroom. Her appearance is that of a ravaged woman. She leans exhaustedly in the doorway, hands clasped over her flat, virginal bosom.*]

MISS COLLINS [*breathlessly*]: Oh, Richard—Richard . . .

PORTER [*coughing*]: Miss—Collins.

ELEVATOR BOY: Hello, Miss Collins.

MISS COLLINS [*just noticing the men*]: Goodness! You've arrived already! Mother didn't tell me you were here! [*Self-consciously she touches her ridiculous corkscrew curls with the faded pink ribbon tied through them. Her manner becomes that of a slightly coquettish but prim little Southern belle.*] I must ask you gentlemen to excuse the terrible disorder.

PORTER: That's all right, Miss Collins.

114

MISS COLLINS: It's the maid's day off. Your No'thern girls receive such excellent domestic training, but in the South it was never considered essential for a girl to have anything but prettiness and charm! [*She laughs girlishly.*] Please do sit down. Is it too close? Would you like a window open?

PORTER: No, Miss Collins.

MISS COLLINS [*advancing with delicate grace to the sofa*]: Mother will bring in something cool after while. . . . Oh, my! [*She touches her forehead.*]

PORTER [*kindly*]: Is anything wrong, Miss Collins?

MISS COLLINS: Oh, no, no, thank you, nothing! My head is a little bit heavy. I'm always a little bit—malarial—this time of year! [*She sways dizzily as she starts to sink down on the sofa.*]

PORTER [*helping her*]: Careful there, Miss Collins.

MISS COLLINS [*vaguely*]: Yes, it is, I hadn't noticed before. [*She peers at them nearsightedly with a hesitant smile.*] You gentlemen have come from the church?

PORTER: No, ma'am. I'm Nick, the porter, Miss Collins, and this boy here is Frank that runs the elevator.

MISS COLLINS [*stiffening a little*]: Oh? . . . I don't understand.

PORTER [*gently*]: Mr. Abrams just asked me to drop in here an' see if you was getting along all right.

MISS COLLINS: Oh! Then he must have informed you of what's been going on in here!

PORTER: He mentioned some kind of—disturbance.

115

MISS COLLINS: Yes! Isn't it outrageous? But it mustn't go any further, you understand. I mean you mustn't repeat it to other people.

PORTER: No, I wouldn't say nothing.

MISS COLLINS: Not a word of it, please!

ELEVATOR BOY: Is the man still here, Miss Collins?

MISS COLLINS: Oh, no. No, he's gone now.

ELEVATOR BOY: How did he go, out the bedroom window, Miss Collins?

MISS COLLINS [*vaguely*]: Yes. . . .

ELEVATOR BOY: I seen a guy that could do that once. He crawled straight up the side of the building. They called him The Human Fly! Gosh, that's a wonderful publicity angle, Miss Collins—"Beautiful Young Society Lady Raped by The Human Fly!"

PORTER [*nudging him sharply*]: Git back in your cracker box!

MISS COLLINS: Publicity? No! It would be so humiliating! Mr. Abrams surely hasn't reported it to the papers!

PORTER: No, ma'am. Don't listen to this smarty pants.

MISS COLLINS [*touching her curls*]: Will pictures be taken, you think? There's one of him on the mantel.

ELEVATOR BOY [*going to the mantel*]: This one here, Miss Collins?

116

MISS COLLINS: Yes. Of the Sunday School faculty picnic. I had the little kindergarteners that year and he had the older boys. We rode in the cab of a railroad locomotive from Webb to Crystal Springs. [*She covers her ears with a girlish grimace and toss of her curls.*] Oh, how the steamwhistle blew! Blew! [*giggling*] *Blewwwww!* It frightened me so, he put his arm round my shoulders! But she was there, too, though she had no business being. She grabbed his hat and stuck it on the back of her head and they—they *rassled* for it, they actually *rassled* together! Everyone said it was *shameless!* Don't you think that it was?

PORTER: Yes, Miss Collins.

MISS COLLINS: That's the picture, the one in the silver frame up there on the mantel. We cooled the watermelon in the springs and afterwards played games. She hid somewhere and he took ages to find her. It got to be dark and he hadn't found her yet and everyone whispered and giggled about it and finally they came back together—her hangin' on to his arm like a common little strumpet—and Daisy Belle Huston shrieked out, "Look, everybody, the seat of Evelyn's skirt!" It was—covered with—grass-stains! Did you ever hear of anything as outrageous? It didn't faze her, though, she laughed like it was something very, very amusing! Rather *triumphant* she was!

ELEVATOR BOY: Which one is him, Miss Collins?

MISS COLLINS: The tall one in the blue shirt holding onto one of my curls. He loved to play with them.

ELEVATOR BOY: Quite a Romeo—1910 model, huh?

MISS COLLINS [*vaguely*]: Do you? It's nothing, really, but I like the lace on the collar. I said to Mother, "Even if I don't wear it, Mother, it will be *so* nice for my hope chest!"

117

ELEVATOR BOY: How was he dressed tonight when he climbed into your balcony, Miss Collins?

MISS COLLINS: Pardon?

ELEVATOR BOY: Did he still wear that nifty little stick-candy-striped blue shirt with the celluloid collar?

MISS COLLINS: He hasn't changed.

ELEVATOR BOY: Oughta be easy to pick him up in that. What color pants did he wear?

MISS COLLINS [*vaguely*]: I don't remember.

ELEVATOR BOY: Maybe he didn't wear any. Shimmied out of 'em on the way up the wall! You could get him on grounds of indecent exposure, Miss Collins!

PORTER [*grasping his arm*]: Cut that or git back in your cage! Understand?

ELEVATOR BOY [*snickering*]: Take it easy. She don't hear a thing.

PORTER: Well, you keep a decent tongue or get to hell out. Miss Collins here is a lady. You understand that?

ELEVATOR BOY: Okay. She's Shoiley Temple.

PORTER: She's a *lady!*

ELEVATOR BOY: Yeah! [*He returns to the gramophone and looks through the records.*]

MISS COLLINS: I really shouldn't have created this disturbance. When the officers come I'll have to explain that to them. But you can understand my feelings, can't you?

118

PORTER: Sure, Miss Collins.

MISS COLLINS: When men take advantage of common white-trash women who smoke in public there is probably some excuse for it, but when it occurs to a lady who is single and always com*pletely* above reproach in her moral behavior, there's really nothing to do but call for police protection! Unless of course the girl is fortunate enough to have a father and brothers who can take care of the matter privately without any scandal.

PORTER: Sure. That's right, Miss Collins.

MISS COLLINS: Of course it's bound to cause a great deal of very disagreeable talk. Especially 'round the *church!* Are you gentlemen Episcopalian?

PORTER: No, ma'am. Catholic, Miss Collins.

MISS COLLINS: Oh. Well, I suppose you know in England we're known as the English Catholic church. We have direct Apostolic succession through St. Paul who christened the Early Angles—which is what the original English people were called—and established the English branch of the Catholic church over there. So when you hear ignorant people claim that our church was founded by—by Henry the *Eighth*—that horrible, *lech*erous old man who had so many wives—as many as *Blue*beard they say!—you can see how ridiculous it *is* and how thoroughly ob*nox*ious to anybody who really *knows* and under*stands* Church *His*tory!

PORTER [*comfortingly*]: Sure, Miss Collins. Everybody knows that.

MISS COLLINS: I wish they *did*, but they need to be in*struc*ted! Before he died, my father was Rector at the Church of St. Michael and St. George at Glorious Hill, Mississippi. . . . I've literally grown up right in the very *shadow* of the Episcopal

119

church. At Pass Christian and Natchez, Biloxi, Gulfport, Port Gibson, Columbus and Glorious Hill! (*with gentle, bewildered sadness*) But you know I sometimes suspect that there has been some kind of spiritual schism in the modern church. These northern dioceses have completely departed from the good old church traditions. For instance our Rector at the Church of the Holy Communion has never darkened my door. It's a fashionable church and he's terribly busy, but even so you'd think he might have time to make a stranger in the congregation feel at home. But he doesn't though! Nobody seems to have the time any more. . . . [*She grows more excited as her mind sinks back into illusion.*] I ought not to mention this, but do you know they actually take a malicious de*light* over there at the Holy Communion—where I've recently transferred my letter—in what's been going on here at night in this apartment? *Yes!!* [*She laughs wildly and throws up her hands.*] They take a malicious de-*LIGHT* in it!! [*She catches her breath and gropes vaguely about her wrapper.*]

PORTER: You lookin' for somethin', Miss Collins?

MISS COLLINS: My—handkerchief . . . [*She is blinking her eyes against tears.*]

PORTER [*removing a rag from his pocket*]: Here. Use this, Miss Collins. It's just a rag but it's clean, except along that edge where I wiped off the phonograph handle.

MISS COLLINS: Thanks. You gentlemen are very kind. Mother will bring in something cool after while. . . .

ELEVATOR BOY [*placing a record on machine*]: This one is got some kind of foreign title. [*The record begins to play Tschaikovsky's "None But the Lonely Heart."*]

MISS COLLINS [*stuffing the rag daintily in her bosom*]: Excuse me, please. Is the weather nice outside?

PORTER [*huskily*]: Yes, it's nice, Miss Collins.

MISS COLLINS [*dreamily*]: So wa'm for this time of year. I wore my little astrakhan cape to service but had to *carry* it *home*, as the weight of it actually seemed *oppres*sive to me. [*Her eyes fall shut.*] The sidewalks seem so dreadfully long in summer. . . .

ELEVATOR BOY: This ain't summer, Miss Collins.

MISS COLLINS [*dreamily*]: I used to think I'd never get to the end of that last block. And that's the block where all the trees went down in the big tornado. The walk is simply *glit*tering with sunlight. [*Pressing her eyelids*] Impossible to shade your face and I *do* perspire so freely! [*She touches her forehead daintily with the rag.*] Not a branch, not a leaf to give you a little protection! You simply *have* to en*dure* it. Turn your hideous red face away from all the front porches and walk as fast as you decently *can* till you get *by* them! Oh, dear, dear Savior, sometimes you're not so lucky and you *meet* people and have to *smile!* You can't *avoid* them unless you cut *across* and that's so *ob*vious, you know. . . . People would say you're pe-*cul*iar. . . . His house is right in the middle of that awful leaf-less block, *their* house, his and *hers*, and they have an auto-mobile and always get home early and sit on the porch and *watch* me walking by—Oh, Father in Heaven—with a ma*l*icious de*light!* [*She averts her face in remembered torture.*] She has such *penetrating* eyes, they look straight through me. She sees that terrible choking thing in my throat and the pain I have in *here*—[*touching her chest*]—and she points it out and laughs and whispers to him, "There she goes with her shiny big red nose, the poor old maid—that *loves* you!" [*She chokes and hides her face in the rag.*]

PORTER: Maybe you better forget all that, Miss Collins.

121

MISS COLLINS: Never, never forget it! Never, never! I left my parasol once—the one with long white fringe that belonged to Mother—I left it behind in the cloakroom at the church so I didn't have anything to cover my face with when I walked by, and I couldn't turn back either, with all those people behind me—giggling back of me, poking fun at my clothes! Oh, dear, dear! I had to walk straight forward—past the last elm tree and into that *merciless* sunlight. Oh! It beat down on me, *scorching* me! *Whips!* . . . Oh, Jesus! . . . Over my face and my body! . . . I tried to walk on fast but was dizzy and they kept closer behind me—! I stumbled, I nearly fell, and all of them burst out laughing! My face turned so *horribly* red, it got so red and wet, I knew how ugly it was in all that merciless glare—not a single shadow to hide in! And then—[*Her face contorts with fear.*]— their automobile drove up in front of their house, right where I had to pass by it, and *she* stepped out, in white, so fresh and easy, her stomach round with a baby, the first of the *six*. Oh, God! . . . And he stood smiling behind her, white and easy and cool, and they stood there waiting for me. *Waiting!* I had to keep on. What else could I do? I couldn't turn *back*, could I? *No!* I said dear *God*, strike me *dead!* He didn't, though. I put my head way down like I couldn't see them! You know what she did? She stretched out her hand to *stop* me! And *he*—he stepped up straight in front of me, *smiling*, blocking the walk with his terrible big white body! "*Lucretia*," he said, "Lucretia *Collins!*" I—I tried to speak but I couldn't, the breath went out of my body! I covered my face and—ran! . . . Ran! . . . *Ran!* [*beating the arm of the sofa*] Till I reached the end of the block—and the elm trees—*started* again. . . . Oh, Merciful Christ in Heaven, how *kind* they were! [*She leans back exhaustedly, her hand relaxed on sofa. She pauses and the music ends.*] I said to Mother, "Mother, we've got to leave town!" We *did* after that. And now after all these years he's finally remembered and come *back!* Moved away from that house and the woman and come *here*—I saw him in the back of the church one day. I wasn't sure—but it *was*. The night after that was the night that he first broke in—and indulged his senses with me. . . . He doesn't realize that I've changed, that I can't feel again the way that I used to feel, now that he's got six children by that Cincinnati girl—three in high school already! Six! Think of that? Six children! I don't know what he'll say when he knows another one's coming! He'll probably blame *me* for it because a man always *does!* In spite of the fact that he *forced* me!

ELEVATOR BOY [*grinning*]: Did you say—a *baby*, Miss Collins?

MISS COLLINS [*lowering her eyes but speaking with tenderness and pride*]: Yes—I'm expecting a *child*.

ELEVATOR BOY: *Jeez!* [*He claps his hand over his mouth and turns away quickly.*]

MISS COLLINS: Even if it's not legitimate, I think it has a perfect right to its father's name—don't you?

PORTER: Yes. Sure, Miss Collins.

MISS COLLINS: A child is innocent and pure. No matter how it's conceived. And it must *not* be made to suffer! So I intend to dispose of the little property Cousin Ethel left me and give the child a private education where it won't come under the evil influence of the Christian church! I want to make sure that it doesn't grow up in the shadow of the cross and then have to walk along blocks that scorch you with terrible sunlight! [*The elevator buzzer sounds from the hall.*]

PORTER: Frank! Somebody wants to come up. [*The Elevator Boy goes out. The elevator door bangs shut. The Porter clears his throat.*] Yes, it'd be better—to go off some place else.

MISS COLLINS: If only I had the courage—but I don't. I've grown so used to it here, and people outside—it's always so *hard* to *face* them!

PORTER: Maybe you won't—have to face nobody, Miss Collins. [*The elevator door clangs open.*]

MISS COLLINS [*rising fearfully*]: Is someone coming—here?

PORTER: You just take it easy, Miss Collins.

MISS COLLINS: If that's the officers coming for Richard, tell them to go away. I've decided not to prosecute Mr. Martin. [*Mr. Abrams enters with the Doctor and the Nurse. The Elevator Boy gawks from the doorway. The Doctor is the weary, professional type, the Nurse hard and efficient. Mr. Abrams is a small, kindly person, sincerely troubled by the situation.*]

MISS COLLINS [*shrinking back, her voice faltering*]: I've decided not to—prosecute Mr. Martin . . .

DOCTOR: Miss Collins?

MR. ABRAMS [*with attempted heartiness*]: Yes, this is the lady you wanted to meet, Dr. White.

DOCTOR: Hmmm. [*briskly to the Nurse*] Go in her bedroom and get a few things together.

NURSE: Yes, sir. [*She goes quickly across to the bedroom.*]

MISS COLLINS [*fearfully shrinking*]: Things?

DOCTOR: Yes, Miss Tyler will help you pack up an overnight bag. [*smiling mechanically*] A strange place always seems more homelike the first few days when we have a few of our little personal articles around us.

MISS COLLINS: A strange—place?

DOCTOR [*carelessly, making a memorandum*]: Don't be disturbed, Miss Collins.

MISS COLLINS: I know! [*Excitedly*] You're come from the Holy Communion to place me under arrest! On moral charges!

MR. ABRAMS: Oh, no, Miss Collins, you got the wrong idea. This is a doctor who—

DOCTOR [*impatiently*]: Now, now, you're just going away for a while till things get straightened out. [*He glances at his watch.*] Two-twenty-five! Miss Tyler?

NURSE: Coming!

MISS COLLINS [*with slow and sad comprehension*]: Oh. . . . I'm going away. . . .

MR. ABRAMS: She was always a lady, Doctor, such a perfect lady.

DOCTOR: Yes. No doubt.

MR. ABRAMS: It seems too bad!

MISS COLLINS: Let me—write him a note. A pencil? Please?

MR. ABRAMS: Here, Miss Collins. [*She takes the pencil and crouches over the table. The Nurse comes out with a hard, forced smile, carrying a suitcase.*]

DOCTOR: Ready, Miss Tyler?

NURSE: All ready, Dr. White. [*She goes up to Miss Collins.*] Come along, dear, we can tend to that later!

125

MR. ABRAMS [*sharply*]: Let her finish the note!

MISS COLLINS [*straightening with a frightened smile*]: It's—finished.

NURSE: All right, dear, come along. [*She propels her firmly toward the door.*]

MISS COLLINS [*turning suddenly back*]: Oh, Mr. Abrams!

MR. ABRAMS: Yes, Miss Collins?

MISS COLLINS: If he should come again—and find me gone—I'd rather you didn't tell him—about the baby. . . . I think it's better for *me* to tell him *that*. [*Gently smiling*] You know how men *are*, don't you?

MR. ABRAMS: Yes, Miss Collins.

PORTER: Goodbye, Miss Collins. [*The Nurse pulls firmly at her arm. She smiles over her shoulder with a slight apologetic gesture.*]

MISS COLLINS: Mother will bring in—something cool—after while . . . [*She disappears down the hall with the Nurse. The elevator door clangs shut with the metallic sound of a locked cage. The wires hum.*]

MR. ABRAMS: She wrote him a note.

PORTER: What did she write, Mr. Abrams?

MR. ABRAMS: "Dear—Richard. I'm going away for a while. But don't worry, I'll be back. I have a secret to tell you. Love—Lucretia." [*He coughs.*] We got to clear out this stuff an' pile it down in the basement till I find out where it goes.

PORTER [*dully*]: Tonight, Mr. Abrams?

MR. ABRAMS [*roughly to hide his feeling*]: No, no, not to-night, you old fool. Enough has happened tonight! [*Then gently*] We can do it tomorrow. Turn out that bedroom light—and close the window. [*Music playing softly becomes audible as the men go out slowly, closing the door, and the light fades out.*]

CURTAIN

AUTO-DA-FÉ

A Tragedy in One Act

CHARACTERS

MME. DUVENET

ELOI,* her son

* Pronounced Ell-wah. The part is created for Mr. John Abbott.

The front porch of an old frame cottage in the Vieux Carré of New Orleans. There are palm or banana trees, one on either side of the porch steps: pots of geraniums and other vivid flowers along the low balustrade. There is an effect of sinister antiquity in the setting, even the flowers suggesting the richness of decay. Not far off on Bourbon Street the lurid procession of bars and hot spots throws out distance-muted strains of the jukeorgans and occasional shouts of laughter. Mme. Duvenet, a frail woman of sixty-seven, is rocking on the porch in the faint, sad glow of an August sunset. Eloi, her son, comes out the screendoor. He is a frail man in his late thirties, a gaunt, ascetic type with feverish dark eyes.

Mother and son are both fanatics and their speech has something of the quality of poetic or religious incantation.

MME. DUVENET: Why did you speak so crossly to Miss Bordelon?

ELOI [*standing against the column*]: She gets on my nerves.

MME. DUVENET: You take a dislike to every boarder we get.

ELOI: She's not to be trusted. I think she goes in my room.

MME. DUVENET: What makes you think that?

ELOI: I've found some evidence of it.

MME. DUVENET: Well, I can assure you she doesn't go in your room.

ELOI: Somebody goes in my room and roots through my things.

MME. DUVENET: Nobody ever touches a thing in your room.

ELOI: My room is my own. I don't want anyone in it.

MME. DUVENET: You know very well that I have to go in to clean it.

ELOI: I don't want it cleaned.

MME. DUVENET: You want the room to be filthy?

ELOI: Just don't go in it to clean it or anything else.

MME. DUVENET: How could you live in a room that was never cleaned?

ELOI: I'll clean it myself when cleaning is necessary.

MME. DUVENET: A person would think that you were concealing something.

ELOI: What would I have to conceal?

MME. DUVENET: Nothing that I can imagine. That's why it's so strange that you have such a strong objection to even your mother going into your room.

ELOI: Everyone wants a little privacy, Mother.

MME. DUVENET [*stiffly*]: Your privacy, Eloi, shall be regarded as sacred.

ELOI: Huh.

MME. DUVENET: I'll just allow the filth to accumulate there.

ELOI [*sharply*]: What do you mean by "the filth"?

MME. DUVENET [*sadly*]: The dust and disorder that you would rather live in than have your mother come in to clean it up.

ELOI: Your broom and your dustpan wouldn't accomplish much. Even the air in this neighborhood is unclean.

MME. DUVENET: It is not as clean as it might be. I love clean window curtains, I love white linen, I want immaculate, spotless things in a house.

ELOI: Then why don't we move to the new part of town where it's cleaner?

MME. DUVENET: The property in this block has lost all value. We couldn't sell our place for what it would cost us to put new paint on the walls.

ELOI: I don't understand you, Mother. You harp on purity, purity all the time, and yet you're willing to stay in the midst of corruption.

MME. DUVENET: I harp on nothing. I stay here because I have to. And as for corruption, I've never allowed it to touch me.

ELOI: It does, it does. We can't help breathing it here. It gets in our nostrils and even goes in our blood.

MME. DUVENET: I think you're the one that harps on things around here. You won't talk quietly. You always fly off on some tangent and raise your voice and get us all stirred up for no good reason.

ELOI: I've had about all that I can put up with, Mother.

133

MME. DUVENET: Then what do you want to do?

ELOI: Move, move. This asthma of mine, in a pure atmosphere uptown where the air is fresher, I know that I wouldn't have it nearly so often.

MME. DUVENET: I leave it entirely to you. If you can find someone to make an acceptable offer, I'm willing to move.

ELOI: You don't have the power to move or the will to break from anything that you're used to. You don't know how much we've been affected already!

MME. DUVENET: By what, Eloi?

ELOI: This fetid old swamp we live in, the Vieux Carré! Every imaginable kind of degeneracy springs up here, not at arm's length, even, but right in our presence!

MME. DUVENET: Now I think you're exaggerating a little.

ELOI: You read the papers, you hear people talk, you walk past open windows. You can't be entirely unconscious of what goes on! A woman was horribly mutilated last night. A man smashed a bottle and twisted the jagged end of it in her face.

MME. DUVENET: They bring such things on themselves by their loose behavior.

ELOI: Night after night there are crimes taking place in the parks.

MME. DUVENET: The parks aren't all in the Quarter.

ELOI: The parks aren't all in the Quarter but decadence is. This is the primary lesion, the—focal infection, the—chancre! In medical language, it spreads by—metastasis! It creeps through the capillaries and into the main blood vessels. From there it is spread all through the surrounding tissue! Finally nothing is left outside the decay!

MME. DUVENET: Eloi, you are being unnecessarily violent in your speech.

ELOI: I feel that strongly about it.

MME. DUVENET: You mustn't allow yourself to sound like a fanatic.

ELOI: You take no stand against it?

MME. DUVENET: You know the stand that I take.

ELOI: I know what ought to be done.

MME. DUVENET: There ought to be legislation to make for reforms.

ELOI: Not only reforms but action really drastic!

MME. DUVENET: I favor that, too, within all practical bounds.

ELOI: Practical, practical. You can't be practical, Mother, and wipe out evil! The town should be razed.

MME. DUVENET: You mean this old section torn down?

ELOI: Condemned and demolished!

MME. DUVENET: That's not a reasonable stand.

ELOI: It's the stand I take.

135

MME. DUVENET: Then I'm afraid you're not a reasonable person.

ELOI: I have good precedence for it.

MME. DUVENET: What do you mean?

ELOI: All through the Scriptures are cases of cities destroyed by the justice of fire when they got to be nests of foulness!

MME. DUVENET: Eloi, Eloi.

ELOI: Condemn it, I say, and purify it with fire!

MME. DUVENET: You're breathing hoarsely. That's what brings on asthma, over-excitement, not just breathing bad air!

ELOI [*after a thoughtful pause*]: I *am* breathing hoarsely.

MME. DUVENET: Sit down and try to relax.

ELOI: I can't any more.

MME. DUVENET: You'd better go in and take an amytal tablet.

ELOI: I don't want to get to depending too much on drugs. I'm not very well, I'm never well any more.

MME. DUVENET: You never will take the proper care of yourself.

ELOI: I can hardly remember the time when I really felt good.

MME. DUVENET: You've never been quite as strong as I'd like you to be.

ELOI: I seem to have chronic fatigue.

MME. DUVENET: The Duvenet trouble has always been mostly with nerves.

ELOI: Look! I had a sinus infection! You call that nerves?

MME. DUVENET: No, but—

ELOI: Look! This asthma, this choking, this suffocation I have, do you call that nerves?

MME. DUVENET: I never agreed with the doctor about that condition.

ELOI: You hate all doctors, you're rabid on the subject!

MME. DUVENET: I think all healing begins with faith in the spirit.

ELOI: How can I keep on going when I don't sleep?

MME. DUVENET: I think your insomnia's caused by eating at night.

ELOI: It soothes my stomach.

MME. DUVENET: Liquids would serve that purpose!

ELOI: Liquids don't satisfy me.

MME. DUVENET: Well, something digestible, then. A little hot cereal maybe with cocoa or Postum.

ELOI: All that kind of slop is nauseating to look at!

MME. DUVENET: I notice at night you won't keep the covers on you.

ELOI: I can't stand covers in summer.

MME. DUVENET: You've got to have something over your body at night.

ELOI: Oh, Lord, oh, Lord.

MME. DUVENET: Your body perspires and when it's exposed, you catch cold!

ELOI: You're rabid upon the subject of catching cold.

MME. DUVENET: Only because you're unusually prone to colds.

ELOI [*with curious intensity*]: It isn't a cold! It is a sinus infection!

MME. DUVENET: Sinus infection and all catarrhal conditions are caused by the same things as colds!

ELOI: At ten every morning, as regular as clockwork, a headache commences and doesn't let up till late in the afternoon.

MME. DUVENET: Nasal congestion is often the cause of headache.

ELOI: Nasal congestion has nothing to do with this one!

MME. DUVENET: How do you know?

ELOI: It isn't in that location!

MME. DUVENET: Where is it, then?

138

ELOI: It's here at the base of the skull. And it runs around here.

MME. DUVENET: Around where?

ELOI: Around here!

MME. DUVENET [*touching his forehead*]: Oh! There!

ELOI: No, no, are you blind? I said *here!*

MME. DUVENET: Oh, here!

ELOI: *Yes! Here!*

MME. DUVENET: Well, that could be eyestrain.

ELOI: When I've just changed my glasses?

MME. DUVENET: You read consistently in the wrong kind of light.

ELOI: You seem to think I'm a saboteur of myself.

MME. DUVENET: You actually are.

ELOI: You just don't know. [*darkly*] There's lots of things that you don't know about, Mother.

MME. DUVENET: I've never pretended nor wished to know a great deal. [*They fall into a silence, and Mme. Duvenet rocks slowly back and forth. The light is nearly gone. A distant juke-box can be heard playing "The New San Antonio Rose." She speaks, finally, in a gentle, liturgical tone.*] There are three simple rules I wish that you would observe. One: you should wear undershirts whenever there's changeable weather! Two: don't sleep without covers, don't kick them off in the night! Three:

139

chew your food, don't gulp it. Eat like a human being and not like a dog! In addition to those three very simple rules of common hygiene, all that you need is faith in spiritual healing! [*Eloi looks at her for a moment in weary desperation. Then he groans aloud and rises from the steps.*] Why that look, and the groan?

ELOI [*intensely*]: You—just—don't—*know!*

MME. DUVENET: Know what?

ELOI: Your world is so simple, you live in a fool's paradise!

MME. DUVENET: Do I indeed!

ELOI: Yes, Mother, you do indeed! I stand in your presence a stranger, a person unknown! I live in a house where nobody knows my name!

MME. DUVENET: You tire me, Eloi, when you become so excited!

ELOI: You just don't know. You rock on the porch and talk about clean white curtains! While I'm all flame, all burning, and no bell rings, nobody gives an alarm!

MME. DUVENET: What are you talking about?

ELOI: Intolerable burden! The conscience of all dirty men!

MME. DUVENET: I don't understand you.

ELOI: How can I speak any plainer?

MME. DUVENET: You go to confession!

ELOI: The priest is a cripple in skirts!

MME. DUVENET: How can you say that!

ELOI: Because I have seen his skirts and his crutches and heard his meaningless mumble through the wall!

MME. DUVENET: Don't speak like that in my presence!

ELOI: It's worn-out magic, it doesn't burn any more!

MME. DUVENET: Burn any more? Why should it!

ELOI: Because there needs to be burning!

MME. DUVENET: For what?

ELOI [*leaning against the column*]: For the sake of burning, for God, for the purification! Oh, God, oh, God. I can't go back in the house, and I can't stay out on the porch! I can't even breathe very freely, I don't know what is about to happen to me!

MME. DUVENET: You're going to bring on an attack. Sit down! Now tell me quietly and calmly what is the matter? What have you had on your mind for the last ten days?

ELOI: How do you know that I've had something on my mind?

MME. DUVENET: You've had something on your mind since a week ago Tuesday.

ELOI: Yes, that's true. I have. I didn't suppose you'd noticed . . .

MME. DUVENET: What happened at the post office?

ELOI: How did you guess it was there?

141

MME. DUVENET: Because there is nothing at home to explain your condition.

ELOI [*leaning back exhaustedly*]: No.

MME. DUVENET: Then obviously it was something where you work.

ELOI: Yes . . .

MME. DUVENET: What was it, Eloi? [*Far down the street a tamale vendor cries out in his curiously rich haunting voice: "Re-ed ho-ot, re-ed ho-ot, re-e-ed!" He moves in the other direction and fades from hearing.*] What was it, Eloi?

ELOI: A letter.

MME. DUVENET: You got a letter from someone? And that upset you?

ELOI: I didn't get any letter.

MME. DUVENET: Then what did you mean by "a letter"?

ELOI: A letter came into my hands by accident, Mother.

MME. DUVENET: While you were sorting the mail?

ELOI: Yes.

MME. DUVENET: What was there about it to prey on your mind so much?

ELOI: The letter was mailed unsealed, and something fell out.

MME. DUVENET: Something fell out of the unsealed envelope?

ELOI: Yes!

MME. DUVENET: What was it fell out?

ELOI: A picture.

MME. DUVENET: A what?

ELOI: A picture!

MME. DUVENET: What kind of a picture? [*He does not an-swer. The jukebox starts playing again the same tune with its idiotic gaiety in the distance.*] Eloi, what kind of a picture fell out of the envelope?

ELOI [*gently and sadly*]: Miss Bordelon is standing in the hall and overhearing every word I say.

MME. DUVENET [*turning sharply*]: She's not in the hall.

ELOI: Her ear is clapped to the door!

MME. DUVENET: She's in her bedroom reading.

ELOI: Reading what?

MME. DUVENET: How do I know what she's reading? What difference does it make what she is reading!

ELOI: She keeps a journal of everything said in the house. I feel her taking shorthand notes at the table!

MME. DUVENET: Why, for what purpose, would she take short-hand notes on our conversation?

ELOI: Haven't you heard of hired investigators?

143

MME. DUVENET: Eloi, you're talking and saying such horrible things!

ELOI [*gently*]: I may be wrong. I may be wrong.

MME. DUVENET: Eloi, of course you're mistaken! Now go on and tell me what you started to say about the picture.

ELOI: A lewd photograph fell out of the envelope.

MME. DUVENET: A what?

ELOI: An indecent picture.

MME. DUVENET: Of whom?

ELOI: Of two naked figures.

MME. DUVENET: Oh! . . . That's all it was?

ELOI: You haven't looked at the picture.

MME. DUVENET: Was it so bad?

ELOI: It passes beyond all description!

MME. DUVENET: As bad as all that?

ELOI: No. Worse. I felt as though something exploded, blew up in my hands, and scalded my face with acid!

MME. DUVENET: Who sent this horrible photograph to you, Eloi?

ELOI: It wasn't to me.

144

MME. DUVENET: Who was it addressed to?

ELOI: One of those—opulent—antique dealers on—Royal . . .

MME. DUVENET: And who was the sender?

ELOI: A university student.

MME. DUVENET: Isn't the sender liable to prosecution?

ELOI: Of course. And to years in prison.

MME. DUVENET: I see no reason for clemency in such a case.

ELOI: Neither did I.

MME. DUVENET: Then what did you do about it?

ELOI: I haven't done anything yet.

MME. DUVENET: Eloi! You haven't reported it to the authorities yet?

ELOI: I haven't reported it to the authorities yet.

MME. DUVENET: I can't imagine one reason to hesitate!

ELOI: I couldn't proceed without some investigation.

MME. DUVENET: Investigation? Of what?

ELOI: Of all the circumstances around the case.

MME. DUVENET: What circumstances are there to think of but the fact that somebody used the mails for that purpose!

ELOI: The youth of the sender has something to do with the case.

MME. DUVENET: The sender was young?

ELOI: The sender was only nineteen.

MME. DUVENET: And are the sender's parents still alive?

ELOI: Both of them still living and in the city. The sender happens to be an only child.

MME. DUVENET: How do you know these facts about the sender?

ELOI: Because I've conducted a private investigation.

MME. DUVENET: How did you go about that?

ELOI: I called on the sender, I went to the dormitory. We talked in private and everything was discussed. The attitude taken was that I had come for money. That I was intending to hold the letter for blackmail.

MME. DUVENET: How perfectly awful.

ELOI: Of course I had to explain that I was a federal employee who had some obligation to his employers, and that it was really excessively fair on my part to even delay the action that ought to be taken.

MME. DUVENET: The action that has to be taken!

ELOI: And then the sender began to be ugly. Abusive. I can't repeat the charges, the evil suggestions! I ran from the room. I left my hat in the room. I couldn't even go back to pick it up!

146

LANDLADY: Nitchevo. That's what he called her. He told me once what it means but I've forgotten. It used to give me a pain.

LITTLE MAN: What?

LANDLADY: I'd come in here to talk. The circumstances I've got to live under are trying. I have a good deal of steam I need to blow off. He was a good listener.

LITTLE MAN: The Russian?

LANDLADY: Sympathetic, but silent. While I talked he was only watching the cat.

LITTLE MAN [*smiling a little*]: And so you don't like her?

LANDLADY: NO. [*She sits comfortably on the bed.*] I'll tell you the story. He was a Russian or something. Polacks I usually call 'em. Occupied this room before he took sick. He'd found the cat in the alley an' brought her home an' fed her an' took care of 'er an' let 'er sleep in his bed. A dirty practice, animals in the bed. Don't you think so? [*The Little Man shrugs.*] Well—the work at the plant is unhealthy for even a strong-bodied man. The Polack broke down. Tuberculosis developed. He gets an indemnity of some kind and goes West. The cat—he wanted to take her with him. I set my foot down on that. I told him she'd disappeared. He left without her. Now I can't get rid of the dirty thing.

LITTLE MAN: The cat?

LANDLADY: Twice today I thrown cold water on her when she come slinking around here looking for him. See how she stares at me? Hatred. Withering hatred. Just like one jealous woman looks at another. I guess she's waiting around for him to come home.

173

LITTLE MAN: Will he?

LANDLADY: Never in this world.

LITTLE MAN: Dead?

LANDLADY: The sixteenth of January I got the notice. Wasn't nobody else to be informed. [*The Little Man nods with a sad smile and strokes the cat.*] Some people say an animal understands. I told her this morning, He ain't coming back, he's dead. But she don't understand it.

LITTLE MAN: I think she does. She's grieving. [*holding her against his ear*] Yes, I can hear her—grieving.

LANDLADY: You're a funny one, too. How does this bedroom suit you?

LITTLE MAN: It's a beautiful room.

LANDLADY: Who're you kidding?

LITTLE MAN: You. How much?

LANDLADY: Three-fifty—in advance.

LITTLE MAN: I will take it, provided—

LANDLADY: What? Provided?

LITTLE MAN: I can do like the Russian and keep the cat here with me.

LANDLADY [*grinning*]: Oh, so you want to do like the Russian.

LITTLE MAN: Yes.

LANDLADY [*fixing her hair at the cracked mirror*]: My husban's a chronic invalid. An injury at the plant.

LITTLE MAN: Yeah? I'm sorry.

LANDLADY: Codeine every day. Fifty cents a pill is what it costs me. I wouldn't mind if only he wasn't such a pill sometimes himself. But who can look at suffering in a person?

LITTLE MAN: Nobody.

LANDLADY: Yes. That's how I feel. Well . . . the Russian used to help me out with man's work in the house.

LITTLE MAN: I see.

LANDLADY: How old are you? I bet I can guess! Thirty-five?

LITTLE MAN: Uh-huh. About.

LANDLADY: Eyetalian?

LITTLE MAN: Uh-huh.

LANDLADY: Wouldn't you think that I was a fortune-teller? My father was a Gypsy. He taught me a lot of the Zigeuner songs. He used to say to me, Bella, you're nine parts music—the rest is female mischief! [*She smiles at him.*] That instrument on the wall's a balalaika. Some night I'll drop in here to entertain you.

LITTLE MAN: Good. I heard you singing as I came up to the house. That's why I stopped. [*She smiles again and stands as if waiting.*]

LANDLADY: I'll call you Musso. Musso for Mussolini. You got a job?

175

LITTLE MAN: Not yet.

LANDLADY: Go down to the plant an' ask for Oliver Woodson.

LITTLE MAN: Oliver Woodson?

LANDLADY: Tell him Mizz Gallaway sent you. He'll put you right on the payroll.

LITTLE MAN: Good. Thanks.

LANDLADY: Linen's changed on Mondays. [*She starts to turn away*.] I got to apologize for the condition the walls are in.

LITTLE MAN: I noticed. Who did it?

LANDLADY: Every man who lived here signed his name.

LITTLE MAN: There must have been a lot.

LANDLADY: Birds of passage. You ever try to count them? Restlessness—changes.

LITTLE MAN [*smiling*]: Yeah.

LANDLADY: You'd think a man with pay-money in his pocket would have something better to do than sign his name on the walls of a rented bedroom.

LITTLE MAN: Is the Russian's name here, too?

LANDLADY: Not his name, he couldn't write—but his picture. There! [*She points to a childish cartoon of a big man*.] Right beside it, *look*—tail—whiskers—the *cat!* [*They both laugh*.] Partners in misery, huh?

LITTLE MAN: A large man?

LANDLADY: Tremendous! But when the disease germ struck him, it chopped him down like a piece of rotten timber . . . Statistics show that married men live longest. I'll tell you why it is. [*She straightens her blouse and adjusts the belt.*] Men that— live by themselves—get peculiar ways. All that part of their lives that was meant to be taken up with family matters is all left over—empty. You get what I mean?

LITTLE MAN: Yeah?

LANDLADY: Well . . . They fill it with makeshift things. I once had a roomer who went to the movies every night of the week. He carried a briefcase with him all of the time. Guess what he carried in it!

LITTLE MAN: What?

LANDLADY: Sanitary paper toilet seats. [*The Little Man looks away in embarrassment.*] A crank about sanitation. Another I had, had a pair of pet bedroom slippers.

LITTLE MAN: Pet—bedroom—?

LANDLADY: Slippers. Plain gray felt, nothing the least bit pic- turesque about them. Only one thing—the odor! Highly objec- tionable, after fifteen years—the length of time I reckon he must 've worn 'em! Well—the slippers disappeared—accidentally on purpose, as they say! Heavens on earth! How did I know he would die of a broken heart? He practickly did! [*She laughs.*] Life was incomplete without those bedroom slippers. [*She turns back to the walls.*] Some day I'm going to take me a wire scrub- bing brush an' a bar of Fels-Naphtha an' leave them walls as clean as they was before the first roomer moved in. [*The door is pushed open. The Old Man enters. He looks like Walt Whitman.*]

OLD MAN: You mustn't do that, daughter.

LANDLADY: Aw. You. Why mustn't I?

OLD MAN: These signatures are their little claims of remembrance. Their modest bids for immortality, daughter. Don't brush them away. Even a sparrow—leaves an empty nest for a souvenir. Isn't that so, young man?

LITTLE MAN: Yes.

OLD MAN: Cataracts have begun to— [*He waves his hand in front of his nearly sightless eyes.*] I'm not sure where you are.

LITTLE MAN [*stretching out his hand*]: Here.

OLD MAN: Be comforted here. For the little while you stay. And write your name on the wall! You won't be forgotten.

LANDLADY: That's enough, now, Father.

OLD MAN: I'm only looking for some empty bottles. Have you any empty bottles?

LANDLADY: How would he have empty bottles? He just moved in.

OLD MAN: I trade them in at the Bright Spot Delicatessen. I'll drop in later to finish our conversation. [*He goes out.*]

LANDLADY: My father-in-law. Don't encourage him, he'll be a nuisance to you. [*She taps her forehead.*] Alcoholic—gone!

LITTLE MAN [*sinking down on the bed and lifting the cat again*]: I'm—tired.

LANDLADY: I hope you'll be comfortable here. I guess that's all.

LITTLE MAN: Oliver Woodson?

LANDLADY [*at the door*]: Oh, yes—Oliver Woodson. [*She goes out. The Little Man rises and removes a stub of pencil from his pocket. Smiling a little, he goes to the wall and beneath the large and elliptical self-portrait of the Russian, he draws his own lean figure, in a few quick pencil scratches. Beneath the cat's picture, he puts an emphatic check mark. Then he smiles at the cat and stands aside to survey.*]

CURTAIN

*It is late one night that winter. The furnished room is empty
except for the cat. Through the frosted panes of the window in
the left wall a steely winter moonlight enters. The window in
the right wall admits the flickering ruddy glow of the plant and
its pulse-like throbbing is heard faintly. The Little Man enters
and switches on the suspended electric globe. He carries a small
package. He smiles at Nitchevo and unwraps the package. It is a
small bottle of cream which he brandishes before her.*

LITTLE MAN: Just a minute. [*He lowers the window shade that
faces the plant.*] Now. We forget the plant. [*He pours the
cream in a blue saucer.*] There. Supper. [*He sets it on the floor
by the bed and sits to watch her eat.*] Nitchevo, don't be nervous. There's nothing to worry about. In winter my hands get
stiff, it makes me clumsy. But I can rub them together, I can
massage the joints. And when the weather turns warmer—the
stiffness will pass away. Then I won't jam up the machine any
more. Today Mr. Woodson got mad. He bawled me out. Because my clumsy fingers jammed the machine. He stood behind
me and watched me and grunted—like this! [*He utters an omi-
nous grunt.*] Oh, it was like a knife stuck in me, between my
ribs! Because, you see, I . . . have to *keep* this job, to provide
the supper. Well . . . I began to shake! Like this! [*He imitates
shaking.*] And he kept standing behind me, watching and grunt-
ing. My hands went faster and faster, they broke the rhythm.
All of a sudden a part was put out of place, the machine was
jammed, the belt conveyor stopped! SCR-E-E-ECH! Every man
along the line looked at me! Up and down and all along the line
they turned and stared—at *me!* Mr. Woodson grabbed me by
the shoulder! "There you go," he said, "you clumsy Dago!
Jammed up the works again, you brainless Spick!" [*He covers
his face.*] Oh, Nitchevo—I lost my dignity—I cried. . . . [*He
draws his breath in a shuddering sob.*] But now we forget about
that, that's over and done! It's night, we're alone together—the

room is warm—we sleep. . . . [*He strips off his shirt and lies back on the bed. There is a knock at the door and he sits up quickly. He makes a warning gesture to the cat. But the caller is not to be easily discouraged. The knock is repeated, the door is thrust open. It is the Landlady in a soiled but fancy negligee.*]

LANDLADY [*resentfully but coyly*]: Oh—you were playing possum.

LITTLE MAN: I'm—not dressed.

LANDLADY: Nobody needs to be bashful on my account. I thought you'd gone out and left on the light in your room. We got to economize on electric current.

LITTLE MAN: I always turn it off when I go out.

LANDLADY: I don't believe you ever go out, except to the plant.

LITTLE MAN: I'm on the night shift now.

LANDLADY: The graveyard shift, they call it. What is the trouble with you and Oliver Woodson?

LITTLE MAN: Trouble? Why?

LANDLADY: I met him in the Bright Spot Delicatessen. "Oh, by way," I said to him, "how's that feller I sent you getting along, that Eyetalian feller?" "Aw, him!" said Mr. Woodson. "Say, what's the matter with him? Isn't he doing okay?" "Naw, he jams things up!" "Well," I said, "give him time, I think he's nervous. Maybe he tries too hard."

LITTLE MAN: What did he say?

LANDLADY: He grunted. [*She smiles. The Little Man pours the rest of the cream in the cat's saucer. He is trembling.*] You

181

must try an' get over being so nervous. Maybe what you need is more amusement. [*She sits on the edge of the bed, with the balalaika.*] Sit back down! There's room for two on this sofa! [*She pats the space beside her. He gingerly sits back down at a considerable distance. His hands knot anxiously together. She plays a soft chord on the balalaika and hums with a sidelong glance at the nervous roomer.*] Tired?

LITTLE MAN: Yes.

LANDLADY: Some nights I hear you—talking through the door. Who is he talking to, I used to wonder. [*She chuckles.*] At first I imagined you had a woman in here. Well, I'm a tolerant woman. I know what people need is more than food and more than work at the plant. [*She plays dreamily for a moment.*] So when I heard that talking I was pleased. I said to myself—"That lonely little man has found a woman!" I only hoped it wasn't one picked up—you know—on the street. Women like that aren't likely to be very clean. Female hygiene's a lot more—complicated. Well . . . [*The Little Man looks down in an agony of embarrassment.*]

LITTLE MAN: It wasn't—a woman.

LANDLADY: I know. I found that out. Just you. Carrying on a one-sided conversation with a cat! Funny, yes—but kind of pitiful, too. You a man not even middle-aged yet—devoting all that care and time and affection—on what? A stray alleycat you inherited just by chance from the man who stayed here before you, that fool of a Russian! The strangest kind of a romance . . . a man—and a cat! What we mustn't do, is disregard nature. Nature says—"Man take woman or—man be lonesome!" [*She smiles at him coyly and moves a little closer.*] Nature has certainly never said, "Man take cat!"

LITTLE MAN [*suddenly, awkwardly rising*]: Nature has never said anything to me.

LANDLADY [*impatiently*]: Because you wouldn't listen!

LITTLE MAN: Oh, I listened. But all I ever heard was my own voice—asking me troublesome questions!

LANDLADY: You hear *me*, don't you?

LITTLE MAN: I hear you singing when I come home sometimes. That's very good, I like it.

LANDLADY: Then why don't you stop in the parlor and have a chat? Why do you act so bashful? [*She rises and stands back of him.*] We could talk—have fun! When you took this room you gave me a false impression.

LITTLE MAN: What do you mean?

LANDLADY: Have you forgotten the conversation we had?

LITTLE MAN: I don't remember any conversation.

LANDLADY: You said you wanted to do just like the Russian.

LITTLE MAN: I meant about the cat, to have her with me!

LANDLADY: I told you he also helped about the house!

LITTLE MAN: I'm on the night shift now!

LANDLADY: Quit dodging the issue! [*There is a pause and then she touches his shoulder.*] I thought I explained things to you. My husband's a chronic invalid, codeine, now, twice a day! Naturally I have—lots of steam to blow off! [*The Little Man moves nervously away. She follows ponderously, reaching above her to switch off the electric globe.*] Now—that's better, ain't it?

LITTLE MAN: I don't think I know—exactly.

183

LANDLADY: You ain't satisfied with the room?

LITTLE MAN: I like the room.

LANDLADY: I had the idea you wasn't satisfied with it.

LITTLE MAN: The room is home. I like it.

LANDLADY: The way you avoided having a conversation—almost ran past the front room every night. Why don't we talk together? The cat's got your tongue?

LITTLE MAN: You wouldn't be talking—to me.

LANDLADY: I'm talking to you—direckly!

LITTLE MAN: Not to *me*.

LANDLADY: You! Me! Where is any third party?

LITTLE MAN: There isn't a second party.

LANDLADY: What?

LITTLE MAN: You're only talking to something you think is me.

LANDLADY: Now we *are* getting in deep.

LITTLE MAN: You made me say it. [*turning to face her*] I'm not like you, a solid, touchable being.

LANDLADY: Words—wonderful! The cat's let go of your tongue?

LITTLE MAN: You're wrong if you think I'm—a person! I'm not—no person! At all . . .

184

LANDLADY: What are you, then, little man?

LITTLE MAN [*sighing and shrugging*]: A kind of a—ghost of a—man . . .

LANDLADY [*laughing*]: So you're not Napoleon, you're Napoleon's ghost!

LITTLE MAN: When a body is born in the world—it can't back out. . . .

LANDLADY: Huh?

LITTLE MAN: But sometimes—

LANDLADY: What?

LITTLE MAN [*with a bewildered gesture*]: The body is only—a shell. It may be alive—when what's inside—is too afraid to come out! It stays locked up and alone! Single! Private! That's how it is—with me. You're not talking to me—but just what you *think* is me!

LANDLADY [*laughing gently*]: Such a lot of words. You've thrown me the dictionary. All you needed to say was that you're lonesome. [*She touches his shoulder.*] Plain old lonesomeness, that's what's the matter with you! [*He turns to her and she gently touches his face.*] Nature says, "Don't be lonesome!" [*The curtain begins to fall.*] Nature says—"*Don't*—be lonesome!"

CURTAIN

It is again late at night. The Little Man enters with snow on his turned up collar and knitted black wool cap.

He carries the usual little package of cream for his friend the cat. Again he follows his nightly routine of lowering the shade on the glare of the plant, pouring the cream in the blue saucer, and the sighing relaxation on the bed.

LITTLE MAN: Nitchevo—don't worry—don't be nervous! [*A needless admonition for Nitchevo doesn't have a care in the world. The Little Man, smiling, watches her as he half-reclines on the bed.*] As long as we stick together there's nothing to fear. There's only danger when two who belong to each other get separated. We won't get separated—never! Will we? [*There is a rap at the door.*] Bella? [*The door is pushed open and the Old Man steps inside.*]

OLD MAN: May I come in? [*The Little Man nods.*] Don't mention this visit to my daughter-in-law. She doesn't approve of my having social relations with her roomers. Where is a chair?

LITTLE MAN [*shoving one toward him*]: Here.

OLD MAN: Thank you. I won't stay long.

LITTLE MAN: You may stay as long as you wish.

OLD MAN: That's very generous of you. But I won't do it. I know how tiresome I am, a tiresome old man who makes his need of companionship a nuisance. I don't suppose you—have a little tobacco?

LITTLE MAN [*producing some*]: Yes—here. Shall I roll it for you?

OLD MAN: Oh, no, no, no. I have a wonderful lightness in my fingers!

LITTLE MAN: Mine shake, they're always clumsy.

OLD MAN: Yes. I understand that. So I—dropped in. I thought we would have a talk.

LITTLE MAN [*embarrassed*]: I don't—talk much.

OLD MAN: Fools hate silence. I like it. I see you have books. From the public library?

LITTLE MAN: One or two. I own them.

OLD MAN: As I was passing outside, I heard some clinking.

LITTLE MAN: Clinking?

OLD MAN: Yes—like bottles. I collect empty bottles which I exchange at the Bright Spot Delicatessen.

LITTLE MAN: The bottle you heard was only a little cream bottle. It's under the bed.

OLD MAN: Oh. That wouldn't do any good. You drink cream?

LITTLE MAN: The cat.

OLD MAN [*nodding*]: Ohhh, so the cat is present! That's what made the air in the room so soft and full of sweetness! Nitchevo —where are you?

LITTLE MAN: She's having her supper.

OLD MAN: Well, I won't disturb her until she's finished. You are devoted to animals?

187

LITTLE MAN: To Nitchevo.

OLD MAN: Be careful.

LITTLE MAN: Of what?

OLD MAN: You may *lose* her. That's the trouble with love, the chance of loss.

LITTLE MAN: Nitchevo wouldn't leave me.

OLD MAN: Not on purpose, maybe. But life is full of accidents, chances, possibilities—not all of which are always very good ones. Do you know that?

LITTLE MAN: Yes.

OLD MAN: A truck might run her down.

LITTLE MAN: Nitchevo was brought up on the street.

OLD MAN: The luxuries of her present existence may have dulled her faculties a little.

LITTLE MAN: You don't understand Nitchevo. She hasn't forgotten how dangerous life can be for a lonely person.

OLD MAN: But she hasn't control of the universe in her hands!

LITTLE MAN: No. Why should she?

OLD MAN: Other things might happen. You work at the plant?

LITTLE MAN: Yes.

OLD MAN [*a fanatical light coming into his clouded eyes*]: Uh-huh! I know those fellows that operate the plant, I know the

188

bosses. They *know* I know them, too. They know I know their tricks. That's why they hate me. Look. Suppose the demand for what they make slacked off. There's two things they could do. They could cut down on the price and so put the product within the purchasing power of more consumers. Listen! I've read books on the subject! But, no! There's another thing they could do. They could cut down on the number of things they make—create a scarcity! See? And boost the price still higher! And so maintain the rich man's margin of profit! Which do you think they'd do? Why, God Almighty—*Nitchevo* knows the answer! They'd do what they've always done. [*He chuckles and rises and begins to sing in a hoarse cracked voice.*]

> Hold up, hold up the Profit,
> Ye Minions of the Boss!
> Lift high the Royal Profit,
> It must not suffer loss!

[*There is a pounding on the wall and vocal objection outside.*]

LITTLE MAN: Mrs. O'Fallon—disturbed.

OLD MAN: Yes, yes! What they'll cut down is production. Less and less men will be needed to run the machines. Fewer and fewer will stand at the belt conveyor. More and more workers will fall into the hands of the social agencies. Independence goes—then pride—then hope. Finally even the ability of the heart to feel shame or despair or anything at all—goes, too. What's left? A creature like me. Whose need of companionship has become a nuisance to people. Well, somewhere along the line of misadventures—is the cat!

LITTLE MAN: Nitchevo?

OLD MAN [*nodding sagaciously*]: You are not able to buy the cream any more.

189

LITTLE MAN: Well?

OLD MAN: Well, cats are *capricious!*

LITTLE MAN: She isn't a fair-weather friend.

OLD MAN: You think she'd be faithful to you? In adversity, even?

LITTLE MAN: She'd be faithful to me.

OLD MAN [*beaming slowly*]: Good! Good! [*He touches his eyelids.*]. A beautiful trust. A rare and beautiful trust. It makes me cry a little. That's all that life has to give in the way of perfection.

LITTLE MAN: What?

OLD MAN: The warm and complete understanding of two or three in a close-walled room with the windows blind to the world.

LITTLE MAN [*nodding*]: Yes.

OLD MAN [*alternatingly tender and vociferous*]: The roof is thin. Above it, the huge and glittering wheel of heaven which spells a mystery to us. Fine—invisible—cords of wonder—attach us to it. And so we are saved and purified and exalted. We three! You and me and—Nitchevo, the cat! [*He lifts her against his ear.*] Listen! She purrs! Mmm, such a soft and sweet and powerful sound it is. It's the soul of the universe—throbbing in her! [*He hands her back to the Little Man.*] Take her and hold her close! Close! Never let her be separated from you. For while you're together—none of the evil powers on earth can destroy you. Not even the imbecile child which is chance—nor the mad, insatiable wolves in the hearts of men! [*The sound of exterior protest gathers volume. A window bangs open and a*

190

woman shouts for an officer. The Old Man crosses to the window that faces the plant. He raises the blind and the flickering red glare of the pulsing forges shines on his bearded face.] There she is!

LITTLE MAN: The plant?

OLD MAN: Uh-huh. [*in a quiet, conversational tone*] The day before yesterday I went down to the plant. I asked the Superintendent about a job. "Oliver Woodson," I said, "this corporation's too big for me to fight with. I've come with the olive branch. I want a job." "You're too old," he told me. "Never mind," I said, "take down my name!" "But, Pop," he said to me, "you're nearly blind!" "Never mind," I said, "take down my name!" "Okay, Pop," said Mr. Oliver Woodson. "What's your name?" "My name is Man," I said. "My name is Man. Man is my name," I said, "spelt M-A-N." "Okay," said Oliver Woodson. "Where do you live?" "I live on a cross," I said. "On what?" "On a cross! I live on a cross, on a cross! [*His voice rising louder and louder.*] Cupidity and Stupidity, that is the two-armed cross on which you have nailed me! Stupidity and cupidity, that is the two-armed cross on which you have nailed me!"

LITTLE MAN: What did he say, then? The Superintendent?

OLD MAN: The Superintendent? Said, "Hush up, be still! I'll send for the wagon!"

WOMAN ROOMER [*shouting in the hall outside*]: I ain't gonna live in no house with a lunatic! I called the police, he's gonna send for th' wagon!

LITTLE MAN [*sadly*]: She's going to send for the wagon.

OLD MAN: There! You see? I speak for the people. For me, they send for the wagon! Never mind. Take down my name.

191

It's Man! [*He leans out the window and shakes his fist at the plant. The forges blaze higher and their steady pulse seems to quicken with the Old Man's frenzy.*] I see you and I hear you! Boom-boom-boom! The pulse of a diseased heart!

LANDLADY [*in the hall*]: Be still, you drunken old fool, you've woke up the house!

WOMAN ROOMER [*outside*]: Terrible, terrible, terrible! Lunatics in the house!

OLD MAN: A fire-breathing monster you are! But listen to me! Because I'm going to speak The Malediction! Go on, go on, you niggardly pimps of the world! You entrepreneurs of deception, you traders of lies! We stand at bay but we are not defeated. The passion of our resistance is gathering force. We can Boom-Boom, too, we're going to Boom! It's only a little while we give you license! We say, Feed on, Feed on! You race of gluttons! Devour the flesh of thy brother, drink his blood! Glut your monstrous bellies on corruption! And when you're too fat to move—that fist will clench, which is the fist of God—to strike! Strike! *STRIKE!* [*He smashes a pane of the window. At this moment the door is burst open. Light spills in from the hall.*]

WOMAN ROOMER [*outside the doorway*]: Watch out! He'll kill somebody!

LANDLADY: Mrs. O'Fallon, be still, get out of the way! Officer, go on in! [*A police officer enters, followed by the Landlady in a wrapper. A group of frightened roomers, gray and bloodless-looking, huddle behind her in the doorway. The Little Man stands clutching the cat against his chest. The Old Man's rage is spent. He stands with head hanging in the banal glow of the electric bulb which the Landlady switches on.*]

LANDLADY [*to the Old Man*]: Ahh, you drunken old fool, my patience is gone. Officer, take him away. Lock him up till he comes to his senses. [*The officer grasps the Old Man's arm.*]

192

OFFICER: Come along, old man.

WOMAN ROOMER [*in the crowd at the door*]: A dangerous, criminal character!

LANDLADY [*to the group*]: Go on, go on back to your beds. The excitement is over. [*The Old Man seems barely conscious as he is pushed out the door. The others retreat behind him. The Little Man makes a dumb, protesting gesture, still clutching Nitchevo against his chest with one arm. The Landlady slams the door on the others. She turns angrily to face the Little Man.*] You! You're responsible for it! Haven't I told you not to encourage him in his drunken ravings? Well! . . . Why don't you say something? [*She jerks the window down.*] Christ. You're not a man at all, you're a poor excuse. Put down that cat! Throw that animal down! [*She snatches Nitchevo from him and casts her to the floor.*] She hates me.

LITTLE MAN: She doesn't like unkindness. [*He stares at her.*]

LANDLADY [*uneasily*]: Why that look? What's the meaning of it?

LITTLE MAN: I'm not looking at you. I'm looking at all the evil in the world. Turn out the light. I've lived too long in a room that was nothing but windows and always at noon and with no curtains to draw. Turn out the light. [*She reaches slowly above her and switches it off. He suddenly goes to her and plunges his head against her chest.*] O beautiful, cruel Zigeuner! Sing to me, sing to me! Comfort me in the dark!

[*At first she stands stiff and hostile. Then she relents and embraces his crouching body, and begins to sing, softly.*]

CURTAIN

A morning in spring. The branches outside the windows of the furnished room bear delicate new leaves which cast their trembling shadows through the panes. On the white iron bed is seated the Boxer in his undershirt paring his corns with a penknife. With a faint creaking, the door is pushed open. The Little Man comes in. His manner is dazed, he looks as though he had had a long illness.

LITTLE MAN [*faintly*]: *Ni*-tchevo?

BOXER [*grinning*]: Sorry, you've got the wrong party—my name is Bill! [*He points to a space on the wall where his signature is scrawled in great letters. A great X mark has been drawn through the portraits of the Russian, the Cat, and the Little Man.*]

LITTLE MAN: This was—my old room.

BOXER: Well, it ain't any more. Unless the landlady rooked me.

LITTLE MAN: You've—moved in here?

BOXER: Yep. I've hung my boxing gloves on the wall. And there's my silver trophies. [*He points to gloves suspended from a nail and several silver cups on the bureau.*]

LITTLE MAN: There was—a cat.

BOXER: A cat?

LITTLE MAN: Yes.

BOXER: Yours?

LITTLE MAN: Yes. She was mine—by adoption. I thought I might—hoped—find her here.

BOXER [*looking at him with humorous curiosity*]: I can't help you out.

LITTLE MAN: You haven't seen one? A gray one? [*He touches his chest.*] White-spotted?

BOXER: Why, I've seen dozens of cats of every description— [*Away in the house somewhere the Landlady commences to sing one of her haunting Zigeuner songs. As he speaks the Boxer returns to paring his corns with an amiable expression.*]—I've seen gray ones, black ones, white ones, spitted, spotted, and sputted! My relations with cats is strictly—*laissez faire!* Know what that means, buddy? Live and let live—a motto. I've never gone *out* of my way—[*looking up reflectively*]—to *injure* a cat. But when one gets *in* my way, I usually *kick* it! [*The Little Man stares at him speechlessly.*] Any more information I can give you?

LITTLE MAN: You see, I worked at the plant.

BOXER: So?

LITTLE MAN: I was fired, I—couldn't handle the work! My— fingers—froze up on me! On the way home, I—something happened. They took me to the Catholic Sisters of Mercy! [*The Boxer grunts.*] I had no idea how many weeks I was there. Observation—mental. When I got out—I wondered about my cat, and that was only this morning. I've—come to get her.

BOXER: I haven't seen her, buddy.

LITTLE MAN [*desperately*]: She hasn't—climbed in the window?

195

BOXER: No. If she did she wouldn't have got a very cordial reception.

LITTLE MAN: She hasn't—been *around*, then? [*His voice breaks, his lips tremble. The Boxer stares at him incredulously. Suddenly he begins to laugh. Helplessly the Little Man laughs with him, breathlessly and uncontrollably. For several moments they laugh together, then all at once the Little Man's face puckers up. He covers his face and sobs. The Boxer grunts with amazement. This is entirely too much. He strides to the door.*]

BOXER [*shouting*]: Bella! Bella! Hey, Bella! [*The Landlady answers. After a moment or two she appears in the door. Her large simplicity is gone. She has frizzed her hair and has on a tight-fitting dress and flashy jewelry. In her now is a sinister, gleaming richness.*]

LANDLADY: Aw. *YOU.* They tole me you got laid off at th' plant. I'm sorry. The room 'as been taken. It's now occupied by this young gentleman here. Your stuff, your few belongings, are packed in the downstairs closet. On your way out you may as well pick them up. [*The Little Man claws in his pockets and pulls out a large dirty rag. He blows his nose on it.*] I can't afford to let my rooms stay vacant. I got to be practical, don't I? I didn't take you under false pretenses. You must remember the first conversation we had, before you even decided you'd take the room. I told you there wasn't nothing soft in my nature. That I was a character perfectly fair and decent—but not sentimental. It's luck in this world, plain luck—and you've got to buck it!

LITTLE MAN: You—came in, nights and—sang.

BOXER: Huh!

LITTLE MAN [*wonderingly*]: Sang. . . .

LANDLADY: What of it? I gave you free entertainment. But that don't mean I was sentimental about you. [*The Little Man shakes his head.*]

LITTLE MAN: Nothing?

LANDLADY: What?

LITTLE MAN: *Nothing?*

BOXER [*annoyed*]: What is this? What's this going on here? Is this my room or is it somebody else's? [*He grabs his gloves from the wall.*] Return me the fin I paid you and I'll move out!

LANDLADY: Just hold your horses a minute!

BOXER: Mine or his?

LANDLADY: Yours, horse-mouth! Take it easy!

BOXER: Naw, I won't. I don't like this kind of business! I rent a room, I want no crackpot visitors coming an' cryin' over some—cat's disappearance!

LANDLADY: Easy, for God's sake! Is this a national crisis? Mr.— Chile con carne! Whatever it is! Please go.

LITTLE MAN [*recovering his dignity*]: I'm going. I only wanted to ask you. Where is the cat?

LANDLADY [*grandly*]: That question I cannot answer. I turned her out.

LITTLE MAN: When?

LANDLADY: I don't remember. Two or three weeks ago, maybe.

197

LITTLE MAN [*despairingly*]: No!

BOXER: Christ.

LITTLE MAN: No, no, no!

LANDLADY [*angrily, to them both*]: Be still! What do you think I am? The nerve a some people . . . Expeck me to play nurse-maid to a sick alley cat? [*There is a pause.*]

LITTLE MAN: Sick?

LANDLADY: Yes! Whining! Terrific!

LITTLE MAN: What was—the matter with her?

LANDLADY: How should I know? Am I a—*vettinerry?* She cried all night and made an awful disturbance. Yes, like you're making now! I turned her out. And when she come slinking back here, I thrown cold water on her three or four times! Finally, finally, she took no for an answer! That is all I have to say on the subjeck.

LITTLE MAN [*staring at her*]: Mean—ugly—fat! [*He repeats it faster.*] Mean, ugly, fat, mean, ugly, fat! [*She slaps him furiously in the face. The Boxer grabs his shoulders and shoves him out the door with a kick.*]

BOXER: Now, God damn it! A *mad*house!

LANDLADY: Ahhh! Th'—

LITTLE MAN [*screaming through the door*]: *Where* is she? Nitchevo, Nitchevo! Where is she? Where did she go? Nitchevo, Nitchevo! Where!

LANDLADY [*screaming back at him*]: Holy God, what do I care where that dirty cat went! She might've gone to the devil for all I care! Get out of the house and stop screaming! I'll call the police! [*The Little Man does not answer and turns away from the door where the Boxer is blocking him.*]

BOXER: Huh! Yes—a *mad*house.

LANDLADY: Out of his mind. Completely. [*She wipes her face on her sleeve and adjusts her clothes.*] Going? Can you hear?

BOXER: Yeah. Going back downstairs.

LANDLADY: God. I hate for people to make a scene like that. Imagine! Holding me responsible for a sick cat. [*She sniffles a little.*] Mean, ugly, fat. . . . I guess I *am*. But who *isn't?*

[*She sinks exhaustedly on the bed. The Boxer stands at the window rolling a cigarette.*]

BOXER: He's gone out back of the house.

LANDLADY: What's he doing back there?

BOXER: Poking around in the alley and calling the cat. [*The Little Man calls in the distance: "Nitchevo!"*]

LANDLADY: Useless. He'll never find her. [*There is a sudden burst of joyful shouting. The Boxer leans out the window and chuckles. A softer, warmer quality appears in the slanting sunlight. There is distant music.*] Now what's going on?

BOXER: A celebration.

LANDLADY: Celebration of what?

BOXER [*lighting his cigarette and resting a foot on the sill*]: The old crackpot with the whiskers has found the cat.

LANDLADY: Found her? Who did you say?

BOXER: The old man, your father-in-law.

LANDLADY: The old man couldn't have found her! [*She gets up languidly and moves to the window.*] How could he have found her? The old man's blind.

BOXER: Anyhow, he found her. And there they go. [*The Landlady gazes wonderingly out the window. The Boxer slips his arm about her waist. The light is golden, the music is faint and tender.*]

LANDLADY: Well, well, well. And so they are leaving together. The funniest pair of lovers! The ghost of a man—and a cat named Nitchevo! I'm glad. . . . Good-bye! [*The music sounds louder and triumphant.*]

CURTAIN

THE LONG GOOD-BYE

CHARACTERS

JOE

MYRA

MOTHER

SILVA

BILL

FOUR MOVERS

Apartment F, third floor south, in a tenement apartment situated in the washed-out middle of a large mid-western American city. Outside the trucks rumble on dull streets and children cry out at their games in the areaways between walls of dusty-tomato-colored brick. Through the double front windows in the left wall, late afternoon sunlight streams into the shabby room. Beyond the windows is the door to the stair hall, and in the center of the back wall a large door opening on a corridor in the apartment where a telephone stand is located. A door in the right wall leads to a bedroom. The furnishings are disheveled and old as if they had witnessed the sudden withdrawal of twenty-five years of furious, desperate living among them and now awaited only the moving men to cart them away. From the apartment next door comes the sound of a radio broadcasting the baseball game from Sportsman's Park. Joe, a young man of twenty-three, is sitting at a table by the double windows, brooding over a manuscript. In front of him is a portable typewriter with a page of the manuscript in it, and on the floor beside the table is a shabby valise. Joe wears an undershirt and washpants. The noise of the broadcast game annoys him and he slams down the windows, but the sound is as loud as ever. He raises them and goes out the door on the right and slams other windows. The shouting of the radio subsides and Joe comes back in lighting a cigarette, a desperate scowl on his face. Silva, an Italian youth, small, graceful and good-natured, opens the entrance door and comes in. He is about Joe's age. By way of greeting he grins and then takes off his shirt.

JOE: Radios, baseball games! That's why I write nothing but crap!

SILVA: Still at it?

JOE: All night and all day.

SILVA: How come?

JOE: I had a wild hair. Couldn't sleep.

SILVA [*glancing at page in machine*]: You're burning the candle at both ends, Kid . . . [*He moves from the table across the room.*] And in my humble opinion the light ain't worth it. I thought cha was moving today.

JOE: I am. [*He flops in table-chair and bangs out a line. Then he removes the sheet.*] Phone the movers. They oughta been here.

SILVA: Yeh? Which one?

JOE: Langan's Storage.

SILVA: Storin' this stuff?

JOE: Yeh.

SILVA: What for? Why don't you sell it?

JOE: For six bits to the junk man?

SILVA: Store it you gotta pay storage. Sell it you got a spot a cash to start on.

JOE: Start on what?

SILVA: Whatever you're going to start on.

JOE: I got a spot a cash. Mother's insurance. I split it with Myra, we both got a hundred and fifty. Know where I'm going?

SILVA: No. Where?

JOE: Rio. Or Buenos Aires. I took Spanish in high school.

SILVA: So what?

JOE: I know the language. I oughta get on okay.

SILVA: Working for Standard Oil?

JOE: Maybe. Why not? Call the movers.

SILVA [*going to the phone*]: You better stay here. Take your money outa the bank and go on the Project.

JOE: No. I'm not gonna stay here. All of this here is dead for me. The goldfish is dead. I forgot to feed it.

SILVA [*into the phone*]: Lindell 0124. . . . Langan's Storage? This is the Bassett apartment. Why ain't the movers come yet? . . . Aw! [*He hangs up the receiver.*] The truck's on the way. June is a big moving month. I guess they're kept busy.

JOE: I shouldn't have left the bowl setting right here in the sun. It probably cooked the poor bastard.

SILVA: He stinks. [*Silva picks up the bowl.*]

JOE: What uh you do with him?

SILVA: Dump 'im into the tawlut.

JOE: The tawlut's turned off.

SILVA: Oh, well. [*He goes out the bedroom door.*]

JOE: Why is it that Jesus makes a distinction between the goldfish an' the sparrow! [*He laughs.*] There is no respect for dead bodies.

SILVA [*coming back in*]: You are losing your social consciousness, Joe. You should say "unless they are rich"! I read about once where a millionaire buried his dead canary in a small golden casket studded with genuine diamonds. I think it presents a beautiful picture. The saffron feathers on the white satin and the millionaire's tears falling like diamonds in sunlight—maybe a boys' choir singing! Like death in the movies. Which is always a beautiful thing. Even for an artist I'd say that your hair was too long. A little hip motion you'd pass for a female Imp. Cigarette?

JOE: Thanks. Christ!

SILVA: What's the matter?

JOE: How does this stuff smell to you? [*He gives him a page of the manuscript.*]

SILVA: Hmm. I detect a slight odor of frying bacon.

JOE: Lousy?

SILVA: Well, it's not you at your best. You'd better get on the Project. We're through with the city guide.

JOE: What are you going to write next?

SILVA: God Bless Harry L. Hopkins 999 times. Naw . . . I got a creative assignment. I'm calling it "Ghosts in the Old Courthouse." Days when the slaves were sold there! . . . This is bad. This speech of the girl's—"I want to get you inside of my body—not just for the time that it takes to make love on a bed between the rattle of ice in the last highball and the rattle the milkwagons make—"

JOE [*tearing the page from his hands*]: I must've been nuts.

206

SILVA: You must've had hot britches!

JOE: I did. Summer and celibacy aren't a very good mix. Buenos Aires. . . .

1ST MOVER [*from the hall outside*]: Langan's Storage!

JOE [*going to the door*]: Right here. [*He opens the door and the four burly Movers crowd in, sweating, shuffling, looking about with quick, casual eyes.*] Take out the back stuff first, will yuh, boys?

1ST MOVER: Sure.

SILVA: Hot work, huh?

2ND MOVER: Plenty.

3RD MOVER [*walking in hastily*]: "I got a pocketful of dreams!" What time's it, kid?

JOE: Four-thirty-five.

3RD MOVER: We oughta get time an' a ha'f w'en we finish this job. How'd the ball game come out?

JOE: Dunno. [*He watches them, troubled.*]

2ND MOVER: What's it to you, Short Horn? Get busy! [*They laugh and go out the rear corridor. Later they are heard knocking down a bed.*]

SILVA [*noting Joe's gloom*]: Let's get out of this place. It's depressing.

JOE: I got to look out for the stuff.

207

SILVA: Come on get a beer. There's a twenty-six-ounce-a-dime joint open up on Laclede.

JOE: Wait a while, Silva.

SILVA: Okay. [*The Movers come through with parts of a bed. Joe watches them, motionless, face set.*]

JOE: That is the bed I was born on.

SILVA: Jeez! And look how they handle it—just like it was an ordinary bed!

JOE: Myra was born on that bed, too. [*The Movers go out the door.*] Mother died on it.

SILVA: Yeah? She went pretty quick for cancer. Most of 'em hang on longer an' suffer a hell of a lot.

JOE: She killed herself. I found the empty bottle that morning in a wastebasket. It wasn't the pain, it was the doctor an' hospital bills that she was scared of. She wanted us to have the insurance.

SILVA: I didn't know that.

JOE: Naw. We kept it a secret—she an' me an' the doctor. Myra never found out.

SILVA: Where is Myra now?

JOE: Last I heard, in Detroit. I got a card from her. Here.

SILVA: Picture of the Yacht Club. What's she doin'—yachting?

JOE [*gruffly*]: Naw, I dunno what she's doin'. How should I know?

BERTHA [*faintly*]: What is it I got to decide?

GOLDIE: Where you're going from here? [*Bertha looks at her silently for a few seconds.*]

BERTHA: Nowhere. Now leave me be, Goldie. I've got to get in my rest.

GOLDIE: If I let you be, you'd just lay here doin' nothin' from now till the crack of doom! [*Bertha's reply is indistinguishable.*] Liseen here! If you don't make up your mind right away, I'm gonna call the ambulance squad to come get you! So you better decide right this minute.

BERTHA [*her body stiffening slightly at this threat*]: I can't decide nothing. I'm too tired—worn out.

GOLDIE: All right! [*She snaps her purse open.*] I'll take this nickel and I'll make the call right now. I'll tell 'em we got a sick girl over here who can't talk sense.

BERTHA [*thickly*]: Go ahead. I don't care what happens to me now.

GOLDIE [*changing her tactics*]: Why don't you write another letter, Bertha, to that man who sells . . . hardware or something in Memphis?

BERTHA [*with sudden alertness*]: Charlie? You leave his name off your dirty tongue!

GOLDIE: That's a fine way for you to be talking, me keeping you here just out of kindness and you not bringing in a red, white or blue cent for the last two weeks! Where do you—

BERTHA: Charlie's a real . . . sweet. Charlie's a . . . [*Her voice trails into a sobbing mumble.*]

233

GOLDIE: What if he is? All the better reason for you to write him to get you out of this here tight spot you're in, Bertha.

BERTHA [*aroused*]: I'll never ask him for another dime! Get that? He's forgotten all about me, my name and everything else. [*She runs her hand slowly down her body.*] Somebody's cut me up with a knife while I been sleeping.

GOLDIE: Pull yourself together, Bertha. If this man's got money, maybe he'll send you some to help you git back on your feet.

BERTHA: Sure he's got money. He owns a hardware store. I reckon I ought to know, I used to work there! He used to say to me, Girlie, any time you need something just let Charlie know. . . . We had good times together in that back room!

GOLDIE: I bet he ain't forgotten it neither.

BERTHA: He's found out about all the bad things I done since I quit him and . . . come to St. Louie. [*She slaps the bed twice with her palm.*]

GOLDIE: Naw, he ain't, Bertha. I bet he don't know a thing. [*Bertha laughs weakly.*]

BERTHA: It's you that's been writing him things. All the dirt you could think of about me! Your filthy tongue's been clacking so fast that—

GOLDIE: Bertha! [*Bertha mutters an indistinguishable vulgarity.*] I been a good friend to you, Bertha.

BERTHA: Anyhow he's married now.

GOLDIE: Just write him a little note on a postcard and tell him you've had some tough breaks. Remind him of how he said he would help you if ever you needed it, huh?

234

BERTHA: Leave me alone a while, Goldie. I got an awful feeling inside of me now.

GOLDIE [*advancing a few steps and regarding Bertha more critically*]: You want to see a doctor?

BERTHA: No. [*There is a pause.*]

GOLDIE: A priest? [*Bertha's fingers claw the sheet forward.*]

BERTHA: No!

GOLDIE: What religion are you, Bertha?

BERTHA: None.

GOLDIE: I thought you said you was Catholic once.

BERTHA: Maybe I did. What of it?

GOLDIE: If you could remember, maybe we could get some sisters or something to give you a room like they did for Rose Kramer for you to rest in, and get your strength back—huh, Bertha?

BERTHA: I don't want no sisters to give me nothing! Just leave me be in here till I get through resting.

GOLDIE: Bertha, you're . . . bad sick, Bertha!

BERTHA [*after a slight pause*]: Bad?

GOLDIE: Yes, Bertha. I don't want to scare you but . . .

BERTHA [*hoarsely*]: You mean I'm dying?

235

GOLDIE [*after a moment's consideration*]: I didn't say that.

[*There is another pause.*]

BERTHA: No, but you meant it.

GOLDIE: We got to provide for the future, Bertha. We can't just let things slide.

BERTHA [*attempting to sit up*]: If I'm dying I want to write Charlie. I want to—tell him some things.

GOLDIE: If you mean a confession, honey, I think a priest would be—

BERTHA: No, no priest! I want Charlie!

GOLDIE: Father Callahan would—

BERTHA: No! No! I want Charlie!

GOLDIE: Charlie's in Memphis. He's running his hardware business.

BERTHA: Yeah. On Central Avenue. The address is 563.

GOLDIE: I'll write him and tell what condition you're in, huh, Bertha?

BERTHA [*after a reflective pause*]: No. . . . Just tell him I said hello. [*She turns her face to the wall.*]

GOLDIE: I gotta say more than that, Bertha.

BERTHA: That's all I want you to say. Hello from—Bertha.

GOLDIE: That wouldn't make sense, you know that.

BERTHA: Sure it would. Hello from Bertha to Charlie with all her love. Don't that make sense?

GOLDIE: No!

BERTHA: Sure it does.

GOLDIE [*turning to the door*]: I better call up the hospital and get them to send out the ambulance squad.

BERTHA: No, you don't! I'd rather just die than that.

GOLDIE: You're in no condition to stay in the valley, Bertha. A girl in your shape's got to be looked out for proper or anything's likely to happen. [*Outside, in the reception room, someone has started the nickel phonograph. It is playing "The St. Louis Blues." A hoarse male voice joins in the refrain and there is a burst of laughter and the slamming of a door.*]

BERTHA [*after a slight pause*]: You're telling me, sister. [*She elevates her shoulders.*] I know the rules of this game! [*She stares at Goldie with brilliant, faraway eyes.*] When you're out you're out and there's no comeback for you neither! [*She shakes her head and then slowly reclines again. She knots her fingers and pounds the bed several times; then her hand relaxes and slips over the side of the bed.*]

GOLDIE: Now, pull yourself together, Bertha, and I'll have you moved to a nice, clean ward where you'll get good meals and a comfortable bed to sleep in.

BERTHA: Die in, you mean! Help me outa this bed! [*She struggles to rise.*]

GOLDIE [*going to her*]: Don't get excited, now, Bertha.

BERTHA: Help me up. Yes! Where's my kimono?

GOLDIE: Bertha, you're not in any shape to go crawling around out of bed!

BERTHA: Shut up, you damned crepe-hanger! Get Lena in here. She'll help me out with my things.

GOLDIE: What've you decided on, Bertha?

BERTHA: To go.

GOLDIE: Where?

BERTHA: That's my business.

GOLDIE [*after a pause*]: Well, I'll call Lena. [*Bertha has risen painfully and now she totters toward the dresser.*]

BERTHA: Wait a minute, you! Look under that tray. The comb and brush tray. [*She sinks, panting, into a rocker.*] You'll find five bucks stuck under there.

GOLDIE: Bertha, you ain't got no money under that tray.

BERTHA: You trying to tell me I'm broke?

GOLDIE: You been broke for ten days, Bertha. Ever since you took sick you been out of money.

BERTHA: You're a liar!

GOLDIE [*angrily*]: Don't call me names, Bertha! [*They glare at each other. A Girl, in what looks like a satin gymnasium out-*]

fit, appears in doorway and glances in curiously. She grins and disappears.]

BERTHA [*finally*]: Get Lena in here. She won't cheat me.

GOLDIE [*going to the dresser*]: Look, Bertha. Just to satisfy you. See under the tray? Nothing there but an old postcard you once got from Charlie.

BERTHA [*slowly*]: I been robbed. Yes, I been robbed. [*with increasing velocity*] Just because I'm too sick an' tired an' done in to look out for myself, I get robbed! If I was in my strength, you know what I'd do? I'd bust this place wide open! I'd get back my money you stole or take it out of your hide, you old—

GOLDIE: Bertha, you spent your last dime. You bought gin with it.

BERTHA: No!

GOLDIE: It was Tuesday night, the night you got sick, you bought yourself a quart of dry gin that night. I swear you did, Bertha!

BERTHA: I wouldn't believe your dying word on a Bible! Get Lena in here! It's a frame-up! [*She rises and staggers toward the door.*] Lena! Lena! *Get me police headquarters!*

GOLDIE [*alarmed*]: No, Bertha!

BERTHA [*still louder*]: GET ME POLICE HEADQUARTERS! [*Collapsing with weakness against the side of the door, she sobs bitterly and covers her eyes with one hand. The electric phonograph starts again. There is the shuffling of dancers outside.*]

GOLDIE: Bertha, be calm. Settle down here now.

239

BERTHA [*turning on her*]: Don't tell me to be calm, you old slut. Get me police headquarters quick or I'll—! [*Goldie catches her arm and they struggle but Bertha wrenches free.*] I'll report this robbery to the police if it's the last thing I do! You'd steal the pennies off a dead nigger's eyes, that's how bighearted you are! You come in here and try to soft-soap me about priests and confessions and—GET ME POLICE HEADQUARTERS! [*She pounds the wall, and sobs.*]

GOLDIE [*helplessly*]: Bertha, you need a good bromide. Get back in bed, honey, and I'll bring you a double bromide and a box of aspirin.

BERTHA [*rapidly, with eyes shut, head thrown back and hands clenched*]: You'll bring me back my twenty-five dollars you stole from under that comb and brush tray!

GOLDIE: Now, Bertha—

BERTHA [*without changing her position*]: You'll bring it back or I'll have you prosecuted! [*Her tense lips quiver; a shining thread of saliva dribbles down her chin. She stands like a person in a catatonic trance.*] I've got friends in this town. Big shots! [*exultantly*] Lawyers, politicians! *I can beat any God damn rap you try to hang on me!* [*Her eyes flare open.*] *Vagrancy, huh?* [*She laughs wildly.*] That's a laugh, ain't it! I got my constitutional rights!

[*Her laughter dies out and she staggers to the rocker and sinks into it. Goldie watches her with extreme awe. Then she edges cautiously past Bertha and out the door with a frightened gasp.*]

BERTHA: Oh, Charlie, Charlie, you were such a sweet, sweet! [*Her head rocks and she smiles in agony.*] You done me dirt more times than I could count, Charlie—stood me up, married a

240

little choirsinger— Oh, God! I love you so much it makes my guts ache to look at your blessed face in the picture! [*Her ecstasy fades and the look of schizophrenic suspicion returns.*] Where's that hellcat gone to? Where's my ten dollars? Hey, *YOU!!* Come back in here with that money! I'll brain you if ever I catch you monkeying around with any money belonging to me! . . . Oh, Charlie . . . I got a sick headache, Charlie. No, honey. Don't go out tonight. [*She gets up from the rocker.*] Hey, you! Bring me a cold ice pack—my head's aching. I got one hell of a hangover, baby! [*She laughs.*] Vagrancy, huh? Vagrancy your Aunt Fanny! Get me my lawyer. I got influence in this town. Yeah. My folks own half the oil wells in the state of— of—Nevada. [*She laughs.*] Yeah, that's a laugh, ain't it? [*Lena, a dark Jewish girl in pink satin trunks and . blouse, comes in the door. Bertha looks at her with half-opened eyes.*] Who're you?

LENA: It's me, Lena.

BERTHA: Oh. Lena, huh? Set down an' take a load off yer feet. Have a cigarette, honey. I ain't feeling good. There ain't any cigarettes here. Goldie took 'em. She takes everything I got. Set down an'—take a—

LENA [*in doorway*]: Goldie told me you weren't feelin' so good this evening so I thought I'd just look in on you, honey.

BERTHA: Yeah, that's a laugh, ain't it? I'm all right. I'll be on the job again tonight. You bet. I always come through, don't I, kid? Ever known me to quit? I may be a little down on my luck right now but—that's all! [*She pauses, as if for agreement.*] That's all, ain't it, Lena? I ain't old. I still got my looks. Ain't I?

LENA: Sure you have, Bertha. [*There is a pause.*]

BERTHA: Well, what're you grinning about?

LENA: I ain't grinning, Bertha.

BERTHA [*herself slightly smiling*]: I thought maybe you thought there was something funny about me saying I still had my looks.

LENA [*after a pause*]: No, Bertha, you got me wrong.

BERTHA [*hoarsely*]: Listen, sweetheart, I know the Mayor of this God damn little burg. Him and me are like that. See? I can beat any rap you try to hang on me and I don't give a damn what. Vagrancy, huh? That's a sweet laugh to me! Get me my traveling bag, will you, Lena? Where is it? I been thrown out of better places than this. [*She rises and drags herself vaguely about the room and then collapses on bed. Lena moves toward the bed.*] God, I'm too tired. I'll just lay down till my head stops swimming. . . . [*Goldie appears in the doorway. She and Lena exchange significant glances.*]

GOLDIE: Well, Bertha, have you decided yet?

BERTHA: Decided what?

GOLDIE: What you're gonna do?

BERTHA: Leave me be. I'm too tired.

GOLDIE [*casually*]: Well, I've called up the hospital, Bertha. They're sending an ambulance around to get you. They're going to put you up in a nice clean ward.

BERTHA: Tell 'em to throw me in the river and save the state some money. Or maybe they're scared I'd pollute the water. I guess they'll have to cremate me to keep from spreadin' infection. Only safe way of disposin' of Bertha's remains. That's a sweet laugh, ain't it? Look at her, Lena, that slut that calls herself Goldie. She thinks she's bighearted. Ain't that a laugh? The only thing big about her is the thing that she sits on. Yeah, the old horse! She comes in here talking soft about callin' a priest an' havin' me stuck in the charity ward. Not me. None a that stuff for me, I'll tell you!

GOLDIE [*with controlled fury*]: You better watch how you talk. They'll have you in the straitjacket, that's what!

BERTHA [*suddenly rising*]: Get the hell out! [*She throws a glass at Goldie, who screams and runs out. Bertha then turns to Lena.*] Set down and take a letter for me. There's paper under that kewpie.

LENA [*looking on the dresser*]: No, there ain't, Bertha.

BERTHA: Ain't? I been robbed a that, too! [*Lena walks to the table by the bed and picks up a tablet.*]

LENA: Here's a piece, Bertha.

BERTHA: All right. Take a letter. To Mr. Charlie Aldrich, owner of the biggest hardware store in the City of Memphis. Got that?

LENA: What's the address, Bertha?

BERTHA: It's 563 Central Avenue. Got it? Yeah, that's right. Mr. Charlie Aldrich. Dear Charlie. They're fixing to lock me up in the city bughouse. On a charge of criminal responsibility without due process of law. Got that? [*Lena stops writing.*] And I'm as sane as you are right this minute, Charlie. There's nothing wrong with my upper story and there never will be. Got that? [*Lena looks down and pretends to write.*] So come on down here, Charlie, and bail me out of here, honey, for old times' sake. Love and kisses, your old sweetheart, Bertha.

. . . Wait a minute. Put a P.S. and say how's the wife and your— No! Scratch it out! That don't belong in there. Scratch it all out, the whole damn thing! [*There is a painful silence. Bertha sighs and turns slowly on the bed, pushing her damp hair back.*] Get you a clean sheet of paper. [*Lena rises and tears another sheet from the tablet. A young Girl sticks her head in the door.*]

GIRL: Lena!

LENA: Coming.

BERTHA: Got it?

LENA: Yes.

BERTHA: That's right. Now just say this. Hello from Bertha— to Charlie—with all her love. Got that? Hello from Bertha—to Charlie . . .

LENA [*rising and straightening her blouse*]: Yes.

BERTHA: With all . . . her love . . . [*The music in the outer room recommences.*]

CURTAIN

THIS PROPERTY IS CONDEMNED

CHARACTERS

WILLIE, a young girl

TOM, a boy

THIS PROPERTY IS CONDEMNED

*A railroad embankment on the outskirts of a small Mississippi
town on one of those milky white winter mornings peculiar to
that part of the country. The air is moist and chill. Behind the
low embankment of the tracks is a large yellow frame house
which has a look of tragic vacancy. Some of the upper windows
are boarded, a portion of the roof has fallen away. The land is
utterly flat. In the left background is a billboard that says "GIN
WITH JAKE" and there are some telephone poles and a few
bare winter trees. The sky is a great milky whiteness: crows
occasionally make a sound of roughly torn cloth.*

*The girl Willie is advancing precariously along the railroad
track, balancing herself with both arms outstretched, one clutching a banana, the other an extraordinarily dilapidated doll with
a frowsy blond wig.*

*She is a remarkable apparition—thin as a beanpole and dressed
in outrageous cast-off finery. She wears a long blue velvet party
dress with a filthy cream lace collar and sparkling rhinestone
beads. On her feet are battered silver kid slippers with large
ornamental buckles. Her wrists and her fingers are resplendent
with dimestore jewelry. She has applied rouge to her childish
face in artless crimson daubs and her lips are made up in a pre-
posterous Cupid's bow. She is about thirteen and there is something ineluctably childlike and innocent in her appearance despite the makeup. She laughs frequently and wildly and with a
sort of precocious, tragic abandon.*

*The boy Tom, slightly older, watches her from below the em-
bankment. He wears corduroy pants, blue shirt and a sweater
and carries a kite of red tissue paper with a gaudily ribboned tail.*

TOM: Hello. Who are you?

WILLIE: Don't talk to me till I fall off. [*She proceeds dizzily.
Tom watches with mute fascination. Her gyrations grow wider
and wider. She speaks breathlessly.*] Take my—crazy doll—will
you?

TOM [*scrambling up the bank*]: Yeh.

WILLIE: I don't wanta—break her when—I fall! I don't think I can—stay on much—longer—do you?

TOM: Naw.

WILLIE: I'm practically—off—right now! [*Tom offers to assist her.*] No, don't touch me. It's no fair helping. You've got to do it—all—by yourself! God, I'm wobbling! I don't know what's made me so nervous! You see that watertank way back yonder?

TOM: Yeah?

WILLIE: That's where I—started—from! This is the furthest—I ever gone—without once—falling off. I mean it will be—if I can manage to stick on—to the next—telephone—pole! Oh! Here I go! [*She becomes completely unbalanced and rolls down the bank.*]

TOM [*standing above her now*]: Hurtcha self?

WILLIE: Skinned my knee a little. Glad I didn't put my silk stockings on.

TOM [*coming down the bank*]: Spit on it. That takes the sting away.

WILLIE: Okay.

TOM: That's animal's medicine, you know. They always lick their wounds.

WILLIE: I know. The principal damage was done to my bracelet, I guess. I knocked out one of the diamonds. Where did it go?

TOM: You never could find it in all them cinders.

WILLIE: I don't know. It had a lot of shine.

TOM: It wasn't a genuine diamond.

WILLIE: How do you know?

TOM: I just imagine it wasn't. Because if it was you wouldn't be walking along a railroad track with a banged-up doll and a piece of a rotten banana.

WILLIE: Oh, I wouldn't be so sure. I might be peculiar or something. You never can tell. What's your name?

TOM: Tom.

WILLIE: Mine's Willie. We've both got boy's names.

TOM: How did that happen?

WILLIE: I was expected to be a boy but I wasn't. They had one girl already. Alva. She was my sister. Why ain't you at school?

TOM: I thought it was going to be windy so I could fly my kite.

WILLIE: What made you think that?

TOM: Because the sky was so white.

WILLIE: Is that a sign?

TOM: Yeah.

WILLIE: I know. It looks like everything had been swept off with a broom. Don't it?

TOM: Yeah.

WILLIE: It's perfectly white. It's white as a clean piece of paper.

TOM: Uh-huh.

WILLIE: But there isn't a wind.

TOM: Naw.

WILLIE: It's up too high for us to feel it. It's way, way up in the attic sweeping the dust off the furniture up there!

TOM: Uh-huh. Why ain't you at school?

WILLIE: I quituated. Two years ago this winter.

TOM: What grade was you in?

WILLIE: Five A.

TOM: Miss Preston.

WILLIE: Yep. She used to think my hands was dirty until I explained that it was cinders from falling off the railroad tracks so much.

TOM: She's pretty strict.

WILLIE: Oh, no, she's just disappointed because she didn't get married. Probably never had an opportunity, poor thing. So she has to teach Five A for the rest of her natural life. They started teaching algebra an' I didn't give a goddam what X stood for so I quit.

TOM: You'll never get an education walking the railroad tracks.

250

WILLIE: You won't get one flying a red kite neither. Besides . . .

TOM: What?

WILLIE: What a girl needs to get along is social training. I learned all of that from my sister Alva. She had a wonderful popularity with the railroad men.

TOM: Train engineers?

WILLIE: Engineers, firemen, conductors. Even the freight sup'rintendent. We run a boardinghouse for railroad men. She was I guess you might say The Main Attraction. Beautiful? Jesus, she looked like a movie star!

TOM: Your sister?

WILLIE: Yeah. One of 'em used to bring her regular after each run a great big heart-shaped red silk box of assorted chocolates and nuts and hard candies. Marvelous?

TOM: Yeah. [*The cawing of crows sounds through the chilly air.*]

WILLIE: You know where Alva is now?

TOM: Memphis?

WILLIE: Naw.

TOM: New Awleuns?

WILLIE: Naw.

TOM: St. Louis?

251

WILLIE: You'll never guess.

TOM: Where is she then? [*Willie does not answer at once.*]

WILLIE [*very solemnly*]: She's in the bone orchard.

TOM: What?

WILLIE [*violently*]: Bone orchard, cemetery, graveyard! Don't you understand English?

TOM: Sure. That's pretty tough.

WILLIE: You don't know the half of it, buddy. We used to have some high old times in that big yellow house.

TOM: I bet you did.

WILLIE: Musical instruments going all of the time.

TOM: Instruments? What kind?

WILLIE: Piano, victrola, Hawaiian steel guitar. Everyone played on something. But now it's—awful quiet. You don't hear a sound from there, do you?

TOM: Naw. Is it empty?

WILLIE: Except for me. They got a big sign stuck up.

TOM: What does it say?

WILLIE [*loudly but with a slight catch*]: "THIS PROPERTY IS CONDEMNED!"

TOM: You ain't still living there?

WILLIE: Uh-huh.

TOM: What happened? Where did everyone go?

WILLIE: Mama run off with a brakeman on the C. & E. I. After that everything went to pieces. [*A train whistles far off.*] You hear that whistle? That's the Cannonball Express. The fastest thing on wheels between St. Louis, New Awleuns an' Memphis. My old man got to drinking.

TOM: Where is he now?

WILLIE: Disappeared. I guess I ought to refer his case to the Bureau of Missing Persons. The same as he done with Mama when she disappeared. Then there was me and Alva. Till Alva's lungs got affected. Did you see Greta Garbo in *Camille?* It played at the Delta Brilliant one time las' spring. She had the same what Alva died of. Lung affection.

TOM: Yeah?

WILLIE: Only it was—very beautiful the way she had it. You know. Violins playing. And loads and loads of white flowers. All of her lovers come back in a beautiful scene!

TOM: Yeah?

WILLIE: But Alva's all disappeared.

TOM: Yeah?

WILLIE: Like rats from a sinking ship! That's how she used to describe it. Oh, it—wasn't like death in the movies.

TOM: Naw?

WILLIE: She says, "Where is Albert? Where's Clemence?" None of them was around. I used to lie to her, I says, "They send their regards. They're coming to see you tomorrow." "Where's Mr. Johnson?" she asked me. He was the freight sup'rintendent, the most important character we ever had in our rooming house. "He's been transferred to Grenada," I told her. "But wishes to be remembered." She known I was lying.

TOM: Yeah?

WILLIE: "This here is the payoff!" she says. "They all run out on me like rats from a sinking ship!" Except Sidney.

TOM: Who was Sidney?

WILLIE: The one that used to give her the great big enormous red silk box of American Beauty choc'lates.

TOM: Oh.

WILLIE: He remained faithful to her.

TOM: That's good.

WILLIE: But she never did care for Sidney. She said his teeth was decayed so he didn't smell good.

TOM: Aw!

WILLIE: It wasn't like death in the movies. When somebody dies in the movies they play violins.

TOM: But they didn't for Alva.

WILLIE: Naw. Not even a goddam victrola. They said it didn't agree with the hospital regulations. Always singing around the house.

TOM: Who? Alva?

WILLIE: Throwing enormous parties. This was her favorite number. [*She closes her eyes and stretches out her arms in the simulated rapture of the professional blues singer. Her voice is extraordinarily high and pure with a precocious emotional timbre.*]

> You're the only star
> In my blue hea-ven
> And you're shining just
> For me!

This is her clothes I got on. Inherited from her. Everything Alva's is mine. Except her solid gold beads.

TOM: What happened to them?

WILLIE: Them? She never took 'em off.

TOM: Oh!

WILLIE: I've also inherited all of my sister's beaux. Albert and Clemence and even the freight sup'rintendent.

TOM: Yeah?

WILLIE: They all disappeared. Afraid that they might get stuck for expenses I guess. But now they turn up again, all of 'em, like a bunch of bad pennies. They take me out places at night. I've got to be popular now. To parties an' dances an' all of the railroad affairs. Lookit here!

TOM: What?

WILLIE: I can do bumps! [*She stands in front of him and shoves her stomach toward him in a series of spasmodic jerks.*]

TOM: Frank Waters said that . . .

WILLIE: What?

TOM: You know.

WILLIE: Know what?

TOM: You took him inside and danced for him with your clothes off.

WILLIE: Oh. Crazy Doll's hair needs washing. I'm scared to wash it though 'cause her head might come unglued where she had that compound fracture of the skull. I think that most of her brains spilled out. She's been acting silly ever since. Saying an' doing the most outrageous things.

TOM: Why don't you do that for me?

WILLIE: What? Put glue on your compound fracture?

TOM: Naw. What you did for Frank Waters.

WILLIE: Because I was lonesome then an' I'm not lonesome now. You can tell Frank Waters that. Tell him that I've inherited all of my sister's beaux. I go out steady with men in responsible jobs. The sky sure is white. Ain't it? White as a clean piece of paper. In Five A we used to draw pictures. Miss Preston would give us a piece of white foolscap an' tell us to draw what we pleased.

TOM: What did you draw?

WILLIE: I remember I drawn her a picture one time of my old man getting conked with a bottle. She thought it was good, Miss Preston, she said, "Look here. Here's a picture of Charlie Chaplin with his hat on the side of his head!" I said, "Aw, naw, that's not Charlie Chaplin, that's my father, an' that's not his hat, it's a bottle!"

TOM: What did she say?

WILLIE: Oh, well. You can't make a school-teacher laugh.

> You're the only star
> In my blue hea-VEN . . .

The principal used to say there must've been something wrong with my home atmosphere because of the fact that we took in railroad men an' some of 'em slept with my sister.

TOM: Did they?

WILLIE: She was The Main Attraction. The house is sure empty now.

TOM: You ain't still living there, are you?

WILLIE: Sure.

TOM: By yourself?

WILLIE: Uh-huh. I'm not supposed to be but I am. The property is condemned but there's nothing wrong with it. Some county investigator come snooping around yesterday. I recognized her by the shape of her hat. It wasn't exactly what I would call stylish-looking.

TOM: Naw?

WILLIE: It looked like something she took off the lid of the stove. Alva knew lots about style. She had ambitions to be a de-

257

signer for big wholesale firms in Chicago. She used to submit her pictures. It never worked out.

You're the only star
In my blue hea-ven . . .

TOM: What did you do? About the investigators?

WILLIE: Laid low upstairs. Pretended like no one was home.

TOM: Well, how do you manage to keep on eating?

WILLIE: Oh, I don't know. You keep a sharp lookout you see things lying around. This banana, perfectly good, for instance. Thrown in a garbage pail in back of the Blue Bird Café. [*She finishes the banana and tosses away the peel.*]

TOM [*grinning*]: Yeh. Miss Preston for instance.

WILLIE: Naw, not her. She gives you a white piece of paper, says "Draw what you please!" One time I drawn her a picture of— Oh, but I told you that, huh? Will you give Frank Waters a message?

TOM: What?

WILLIE: Tell him the freight sup'rintendent has bought me a pair of kid slippers. Patent. The same as the old ones of Alva's. I'm going to dances with them at Moon Lake Casino. All night I'll be dancing an' come home drunk in the morning! We'll have serenades with all kinds of musical instruments. Trumpets an' trombones. An' Hawaiian steel guitars. Yeh! Yeh! [*She rises excitedly.*] The sky will be white like this.

TOM [*impressed*]: Will it?

WILLIE: Uh-huh. [*She smiles vaguely and turns slowly toward*

him.] White—as a clean—piece of paper . . . [*then excitedly*]
I'll draw—pictures on it!

TOM: Will you?

WILLIE: Sure!

TOM: Pictures of what?

WILLIE: Me dancing! With the freight sup'rintendent! In a
pair of patent kid shoes! Yeh! Yeh! With French heels on them
as high as telegraph poles! An' they'll play my favorite music!

TOM: Your favorite?

WILLIE: Yeh. The same as Alva's. [*breathlessly, passionately*]

> You're the only STAR—
> In my blue HEA-VEN . . .

I'll—

TOM: What?

WILLIE: I'll—wear a corsage!

TOM: What's that?

WILLIE: Flowers to pin on your dress at a formal affair! Rose-
buds! Violets! And lilies-of-the-valley! When you come home
it's withered but you stick 'em in a bowl of water to freshen
'em up.

TOM: Uh-huh.

WILLIE: That's what Alva done. [*She pauses, and in the silence
the train whistles.*] The Cannonball Express . . .

259

TOM: You think a lot about Alva. Don't you?

WILLIE: Oh, not so much. Now an' then. It wasn't like death in the movies. Her beaux disappeared. An' they didn't have violins playing. I'm going back now.

TOM: Where to, Willie?

WILLIE: The watertank.

TOM: Yeah?

WILLIE: An' start all over again. Maybe I'll break some kind of continuous record. Alva did once. At a dance marathon in Mobile. Across the state line. Alabama. You can tell Frank Waters everything that I told you. I don't have time for inexperienced people. I'm going out now with popular railroad men, men with good salaries, too. Don't you believe me?

TOM: No. I think you're drawing an awful lot on your imagination.

WILLIE: Well, if I wanted to I could prove it. But you wouldn't be worth convincing. [*She smooths out Crazy Doll's hair.*] I'm going to live for a long, long time like my sister. An' when my lungs get affected I'm going to die like she did—maybe not like in the movies, with violins playing—but with my pearl earrings on an' my solid gold beads from Memphis. . . .

TOM: Yes?

WILLIE [*examining Crazy Doll very critically*]: An' then I guess—

TOM: What?

260

WILLIE [*gaily but with a slight catch*]: Somebody else will inherit all of my beaux! The sky sure is white.

TOM: It sure is.

WILLIE: White as a clean piece of paper. I'm going back now.

TOM: So long.

WILLIE: Yeh. So long. [*She starts back along the railroad track, weaving grotesquely to keep her balance. She disappears. Tom wets his finger and holds it up to test the wind. Willie is heard singing from a distance.*]

> You're the only star
> In my blue heaven—

[*There is a brief pause. The stage begins to darken.*]

> An' you're shining just—
> For me!

CURTAIN

TALK TO ME LIKE THE RAIN
AND LET ME LISTEN . . .

CHARACTERS

MAN

WOMAN

CHILD'S VOICE (offstage)

TALK TO ME LIKE THE RAIN
AND LET ME LISTEN . . .

A furnished room west of Eighth Avenue in midtown Manhattan. On a folding bed lies a Man in crumpled underwear, struggling out of sleep with the sighs of a man who went to bed very drunk. A Woman sits in a straight chair at the room's single window, outlined dimly against a sky heavy with a rain that has not yet begun to fall. The Woman is holding a tumbler of water from which she takes small, jerky sips like a bird drinking. Both of them have ravaged young faces like the faces of children in a famished country. In their speech there is a sort of politeness, a sort of tender formality like that of two lonely children who want to be friends, and yet there is an impression that they have lived in this intimate situation for a long time and that the present scene between them is the repetition of one that has been repeated so often that its plausible emotional contents, such as reproach and contrition, have been completely worn out and there is nothing left but acceptance of something hopelessly inalterable between them.

MAN [*hoarsely*]: What time is it? [*The Woman murmurs something inaudible.*] What, honey?

WOMAN: Sunday.

MAN: I know it's Sunday. You never wind the clock.

[*The Woman stretches a thin bare arm out of the ravelled pink rayon sleeve of her kimono and picks up the tumbler of water and the weight of it seems to pull her forward a little. The Man watches solemnly, tenderly from the bed as she sips the water. A thin music begins, hesitantly, repeating a phrase several times as if someone in a next room were trying to remember a song on a mandolin. Sometimes a phrase is sung in Spanish. The song could be* Estrellita.]

[*Rain begins; it comes and goes during the play; there is a drumming flight of pigeons past the window and a child's voice chants outside—*]

CHILD'S VOICE: Rain, rain, go away!
Come again some other day!

[*The chant is echoed mockingly by another child farther away.*]

MAN [*finally*]: I wonder if I cashed my unemployment. [*The Woman leans forward with the weight of the glass seeming to pull her; sets it down on the windowsill with a small crash that seems to startle her. She laughs breathlessly for a moment. The Man continues, without much hope.*] I hope I didn't cash my unemployment. Where's my clothes? Look in my pockets and see if I got the cheque on me.

WOMAN: You came back while I was out looking for you and picked the cheque up and left a note on the bed that I couldn't make out.

MAN: You couldn't make out the note?

WOMAN: Only a telephone number. I called the number but there was so much noise I couldn't hear.

MAN: Noise? Here?

WOMAN: No, noise there.

MAN: Where was "there"?

WOMAN: I don't know. Somebody said come over and hung up and all I got afterwards was a busy signal . . .

MAN: When I woke up I was in a bathtub full of melting ice cubes and Miller's High Life beer. My skin was blue. I was gasping for breath in a bathtub full of ice cubes. It was near a river but I don't know if it was the East or the Hudson. People do terrible things to a person when he's unconscious in this city. I'm sore all over like I'd been kicked downstairs, not like I fell but was kicked. One time I remember all my hair was shaved off. Another time they stuffed me into a trashcan in the alley and I've come to with cuts and burns on my body. Vicious people abuse you when you're unconscious. When I woke up I was naked in a bathtub full of melting ice cubes. I crawled out and went into the parlor and someone was going out of the other door as I came in and I opened the door and heard the door of an elevator shut and saw the doors of a corridor in a hotel. The TV was on and there was a record playing at the same time; the parlor was full of rolling tables loaded with stuff from Room Service, and whole hams, whole turkeys, three-decker sandwiches cold and turning stiff, and bottles and bottles and bottles of all kinds of liquors that hadn't even been opened and buckets of ice cubes melting . . . Somebody closed a door as I came in . . . [*The Woman sips water.*] As I came in someone was going out. I heard a door shut and I went to the door and heard the door of an elevator shut . . . [*The Woman sets her glass down.*]—All over the floor of this pad near the river—articles—clothing—scattered . . . [*The Woman gasps as a flight of pigeons sweeps past the open window.*]—Bras!—Panties!—Shirts, ties, socks—and so forth . . .

WOMAN [*faintly*]: Clothes?

MAN: Yes, all kinds of personal belongings and broken glass and furniture turned over as if there'd been a free-for-all fight going on and the pad was—raided . . .

WOMAN: Oh.

MAN: Violence must have—broken out in the—place . . .

WOMAN: You were—?

MAN: —in the bathtub on—ice . . .

WOMAN: Oh . . .

MAN: And I remember picking up the phone to ask what hotel it was but I don't remember if they told me or not . . .
Give me a drink of that water. [*Both of them rise and meet in
the center of the room. The glass is passed gravely between
them. He rinses his mouth, staring at her gravely, and crosses
to spit out the window. Then he returns to the center of the
room and hands the glass back to her. She takes a sip of the water. He places his fingers tenderly on her long throat.*] Now
I've recited the litany of my sorrows! [*Pause: the mandolin is
heard.*] And what have you got to tell me? Tell me a little
something of what's going on behind your—[*His fingers trail
across her forehead and eyes. She closes her eyes and lifts a hand
in the air as if about to touch him. He takes the hand and ex-
amines it upside down and then he presses its fingers to his lips.
When he releases her fingers she touches him with them. She
touches his thin smooth chest which is smooth as a child's and
then she touches his lips. He raises his hand and lets his fingers
slide along her throat and into the opening of the kimono as the
mandolin gathers assurance. She turns and leans against him, her
throat curving over his shoulder, and he runs his fingers along
the curve of her throat and says—*] It's been so long since we
have been together except like a couple of strangers living together. Let's find each other and maybe we won't be lost. Talk
to me! I've been lost!—I thought of you often but couldn't call
you, honey. Thought of you all the time but couldn't call. What
could I say if I called? Could I say, I'm lost? Lost in the city?
Passed around like a dirty *post*card among people?—And then
hang up . . . I am lost in this—city . . .

WOMAN: I've had nothing but water since you left! [*She says this almost gaily, laughing at the statement. The Man holds her tight to him with a soft, shocked cry.*]—Not a thing but instant coffee until it was used up, and water! [*She laughs convulsively.*]

MAN: Can you talk to me, honey? Can you talk to me, now?

WOMAN: Yes!

MAN: Well, talk to me like the rain and—let me listen, let me lie here and—listen . . . [*He falls back across the bed, rolls on his belly, one arm hanging over the side of the bed and occasionally drumming the floor with his knuckles. The mandolin continues.*] It's been too long a time since—we levelled with each other. Now tell me things. What have you been thinking in the silence?—While I've been passed around like a dirty post-card in this city . . . Tell me, talk to me! Talk to me like the rain and I will lie here and listen.

WOMAN: I—

MAN: You've got to, it's necessary! I've got to know, so talk to me like the rain and I will lie here and listen, I will lie here and—

WOMAN: I want to go away.

MAN: You do?

WOMAN: *I want to go away!*

MAN: How?

WOMAN: *Alone!* [*She returns to window.*]—I'll register under a made-up name at a little hotel on the coast . . .

MAN: What name?

269

WOMAN: Anna—Jones . . . The chambermaid will be a little old lady who has a grandson that she talks about . . . I'll sit in the chair while the old lady makes the bed, my arms will hang over the—sides, and—her voice will be—peaceful . . . She'll tell me what her grandson had for supper!—tapioca and—cream . . . [*The Woman sits by the window and sips the water.*]—The room will be shadowy, cool, and filled with the murmur of—

MAN: Rain?

WOMAN: Yes. Rain.

MAN: And—?

WOMAN: Anxiety will—pass—over!

MAN: Yes . . .

WOMAN: After a while the little old woman will say, Your bed is made up, Miss, and I'll say—Thank you . . . Take a dollar out of my pocketbook. The door will close. And I'll be alone again. The windows will be tall with long blue shutters and it will be a season of rain—rain—rain . . . My life will be like the room, cool—shadowy cool and—filled with the murmur of—

MAN: Rain . . .

WOMAN: I will receive a check in the mail every week that I can count on. The little old lady will cash the checks for me and get me books from a library and pick up—laundry . . . I'll always have clean things!—I'll dress in white. I'll never be very strong or have much energy left, but have enough after a while to walk on the—esplanade—to walk on the beach without effort . . . In the evening I'll walk on the esplanade along the beach. I'll have a certain beach where I go to sit, a little way from the pavillion where the band plays Victor Herbert selections while it gets dark . . . I'll have a big room with shutters on the windows. There will be a season of rain, rain, rain. And I will be so exhausted after my life in the city that I won't mind just listening to the rain. I'll be so quiet. The lines will disappear from my face. My eyes won't be inflamed at all any more. I'll have no friends. I'll have no acquaintances even. When I get sleepy, I'll walk slowly back to the little hotel. The clerk will say, Good evening, Miss Jones, and I'll just barely smile and take my key. I won't ever look at a newspaper or hear a radio; I won't have any idea of what's going on in the world. I will not be conscious of time passing at all . . . One day I will look in the mirror and I will see that my hair is beginning to turn grey and for the first time I will realize that I have been living in this little hotel under a made-up name without any friends or ac- quaintances or any kind of connections for twenty-five years. It will surprise me a little but it won't bother me any. I will be glad that time has passed as easily as that. Once in a while I may go out to the movies. I will sit in the back row with all that darkness around me and figures sitting motionless on each side not conscious of me. Watching the screen. Imaginary peo- ple. People in stories. I will read long books and the journals of dead writers. I will feel closer to them than I ever felt to people I used to know before I withdrew from the world. It will be sweet and cool this friendship of mine with dead poets, for I won't have to touch them or answer their questions. They will talk to me and not expect me to answer. And I'll get sleepy lis- tening to their voices explaining the mysteries to me. I'll fall asleep with the book still in my fingers, and it will rain. I'll wake up and hear the rain and go back to sleep. A season of rain, rain, rain . . . Then one day, when I have closed a book or come home alone from the movies at eleven o'clock at night—I will look in the mirror and see that my hair has turned white. White, absolutely white. As white as the foam on the waves. [*She gets up and moves about the room as she continues—*] I'll run my hands down my body and feel how amazingly light and thin I have grown. Oh, my, how thin I will be. Almost transparent. Not hardly real any more. Then I will realize, I will know, sort of dimly, that I have been staying on here in this little hotel, without any—social connections, responsibilities, anxieties or disturbances of any kind—for just about fifty years. Half a century. Practically a lifetime. I won't even remember the names of the people I knew before I came here nor how it feels to be someone waiting for someone that—may not come . . . Then I will know—looking in the mirror—the first time has come for me to walk out alone once more on the esplanade with the strong wind beating on me, the white clean wind that blows from the edge of the world, from even further than that, from the cool outer edges of space, from even beyond whatever there is beyond the edges of space . . . [*She sits down again unsteadily by the window.*]—Then I'll go out and walk on the esplanade. I'll walk alone and be blown thinner and thinner.

MAN: Baby. Come back to bed.

WOMAN: And thinner and thinner and thinner and thinner and thinner! [*He crosses to her and raises her forcibly from the chair.*]—Till finally I won't have any body at all, and the wind picks me up in its cool white arms forever, and takes me away!

MAN [*pressing his mouth to her throat*]: Come on back to bed with me!

WOMAN: *I want to go away, I want to go away!* [*He releases her and she crosses to center of room sobbing uncontrollably. She sits down on the bed. He sighs and leans out the window, the light flickering beyond him, the rain coming down harder. The Woman shivers and crosses her arms against her breasts. Her sobbing dies out but she breathes with effort. Light flickers and wind whines coldly. The Man remains leaning out. At last she says to him softly—*] Come back to bed. Come on back to bed, baby . . . [*He turns his lost face to her as—*]

THE CURTAIN FALLS

SOMETHING UNSPOKEN

CHARACTERS

MISS CORNELIA SCOTT

MISS GRACE LANCASTER

Miss Cornelia Scott, 60, a wealthy southern spinster, is seated at a small mahogany table which is set for two. The other place, not yet occupied, has a single rose in a crystal vase before it. Miss Scott's position at the table is flanked by a cradle phone, a silver tray of mail, and an ornate silver coffee urn. An imperial touch is given by purple velvet drapes directly behind her figure at the table. A console phonograph is at the edge of lighted area. At rise of the curtain she is dialing a number on the phone.

CORNELIA: Is this Mrs. Horton Reid's residence? I am calling for Miss Cornelia Scott. Miss Scott is sorry that she will not be able to attend the meeting of the Confederate Daughters this afternoon as she woke up this morning with a sore throat and has to remain in bed, and will you kindly give her apologies to Mrs. Reid for not letting her know sooner. Thank you. Oh, wait a moment! I think Miss Scott has another message.

[*Grace Lancaster enters the lighted area. Cornelia raises her hand in a warning gesture.*]

—What is it, Miss Scott? [*There is a brief pause.*] Oh. Miss Scott would like to leave word for Miss Esmeralda Hawkins to call her as soon as she arrives. Thank you. Good-bye. [*She hangs up.*] You see I am having to impersonate my secretary this morning!

GRACE: The light was so dim it didn't wake me up.

[*Grace Lancaster is 40 or 45, faded but still pretty. Her blonde hair, graying slightly, her pale eyes, her thin figure, in a pink silk dressing gown, give her an insubstantial quality in sharp contrast to Miss Scott's Roman grandeur. There is between the two women a mysterious tension, an atmosphere of something unspoken.*]

275

CORNELIA: I've already opened the mail.

GRACE: Anything of interest?

CORNELIA: A card from Thelma Peterson at Mayo's.

GRACE: Oh, how is Thelma?

CORNELIA: She says she's "progressing nicely," whatever that indicates.

GRACE: Didn't she have something removed?

CORNELIA: Several things, I believe.

GRACE: *Oh, here's the "Fortnightly Review of Current Letters!"*

CORNELIA: Much to my astonishment. I thought I had cancelled my subscription to that publication.

GRACE: Really, Cornelia?

CORNELIA: Surely you remember. I cancelled my subscription immediately after the issue came out with that scurrilous attack on my cousin Cecil Tutwiler Bates, the only dignified novelist the South has produced since Thomas Nelson Page.

GRACE: Oh, yes, I do remember. You wrote a furious letter of protest to the editor of the magazine and you received such a conciliatory reply from an associate editor named Caroline Something or Other that you were completely mollified and cancelled the cancellation!

CORNELIA: I have never been mollified by conciliatory replies, never completely and never even partially, and if I wrote to the editor-in-chief and was answered by an associate editor, my reaction to that piece of impertinence would hardly be what you call "mollified."

GRACE [*changing the subject*]: Oh, here's the new catalogue from the Gramophone Shoppe in Atlanta!

CORNELIA [*conceding a point*]: Yes, there it is.

GRACE: I see you've checked several items.

CORNELIA: I think we ought to build up our collection of Lieder.

GRACE: You've checked a Sibelius that we already have.

CORNELIA: It's getting a little bit scratchy. [*She inhales deeply and sighs, her look fastened upon the silent phone.*] You'll also notice that I've checked a few operatic selections.

GRACE [*excitedly*]: Where, which ones, I don't see them!

CORNELIA: Why are you so excited over the catalogue, dear?

GRACE: I adore phonograph records!

CORNELIA: I wish you adored them enough to put them back in their proper places in albums.

GRACE: Oh, here's the Vivaldi we wanted!

CORNELIA: Not "we" dear. Just you.

GRACE: Not *you*, Cornelia?

CORNELIA: I think Vivaldi's a very thin shadow of Bach.

277

GRACE: How strange that I should have the impression you— [*The phone rings.*]—Shall I answer?

CORNELIA: If you will be so kind.

GRACE [*lifting receiver*]: *Miss Scott's* residence! [*This announcement is made in a tone of reverence, as though mentioning a seat of holiness.*] Oh, no, no, this is Grace, but Cornelia is right by my side. [*She passes the phone.*] Esmeralda Hawkins.

CORNELIA [*grimly*]: I've been expecting her call. [*into phone*] Hello, Esmeralda, my dear. I've been expecting your call. Now where are you calling me from? Of course I know that you're calling me from the meeting, *ça va sans dire, ma petite!* Ha ha! But from which phone in the house, there's two, you know, the one in the downstairs hall and the one in the chatelaine's boudoir where the ladies will probably be removing their wraps. Oh. You're on the downstairs', are you? Well, by this time I presume that practically all the daughters have assembled. Now go upstairs and call me back from there so we can talk with a little more privacy, dear, as I want to make my position very clear before the meeting commences. Thank you, dear.

[*She hangs up and looks grimly into space.*]

GRACE: The—Confederate Daughters?

CORNELIA: Yes! They're holding the Annual Election today.

GRACE: Oh, how exciting! Why aren't you at the meeting?

CORNELIA: I preferred not to go.

GRACE: You preferred *not* to go?

CORNELIA: Yes, I preferred not to go . . . [*She touches her chest breathing heavily as if she had run upstairs.*]

GRACE: But it's the annual election of officers!

CORNELIA: Yes! I told you it was! [*Grace drops the spoon. Cornelia cries out and jumps a little.*]

GRACE: I'm so sorry! [*She rings the bell for a servant.*]

CORNELIA: Intrigue, intrigue and duplicity, revolt me so that I wouldn't be able to breathe in the same atmosphere! [*Grace rings the bell louder.*] Why are you ringing that bell? You know Lucinda's not here!

GRACE: I'm so sorry. Where has Lucinda gone?

CORNELIA [*in a hoarse whisper, barely audible*]: There's a big colored funeral in town. [*She clears her throat violently and repeats the statement.*]

GRACE: Oh, dear. You have that nervous laryngitis.

CORNELIA: No sleep, no sleep last night.

[*The phone screams at her elbow. She cries out and thrusts it from her as if it were on fire.*]

GRACE [*picking up the phone*]: Miss Scott's residence. Oh. Just a moment, please.

CORNELIA [*snatching phone*]: Esmeralda, are you upstairs now?

GRACE [*in a loud whisper*]: It isn't Esmeralda, it's Mrs. C. C. Bright!

CORNELIA: One moment, one moment, one moment! [*She thrusts phone back at Grace with a glare of fury.*] How dare you put me on the line with that woman!

GRACE: Cornelia, I didn't, I was just going to ask you if you—

CORNELIA: *Hush!* [*She springs back from the table, glaring across it.*]—Now give me that phone. [*She takes it, and says coldly:*] What can I do for you, please? No. I'm afraid that my garden will not be open to the Pilgrims this spring. I think the cultivation of gardens is an esthetic hobby and not a competitive sport. Individual visitors will be welcome if they call in advance so that I can arrange for my gardener to show them around, but no bands of Pilgrims, not after the devastation my garden suffered last spring—Pilgrims coming with dogs—picking flowers and— You're entirely welcome, yes, good-bye! [*She returns the phone to Grace.*]

GRACE: I think the election would have been less of a strain if you'd gone to it, Cornelia.

CORNELIA: I don't know what you are talking about.

GRACE: Aren't you up for office?

CORNELIA: "Up for office"? What is "up for office"?

GRACE: Why, ha ha!—*running* for—something?

CORNELIA: Have you ever known me to "*run*" for anything, Grace? Whenever I've held an office in a society or club it's been at the *insistence* of the members because I really have an *aversion* to holding office. But this is a different thing, a different thing altogether. It's a test of something. You see I have known for some time, now, that there is a little group, a *clique*, in the Daughters, which is hostile to me!

GRACE: Oh, Cornelia, I'm sure you must be mistaken.

CORNELIA: No. There is a movement against me.

GRACE: A movement? A movement against you?

CORNELIA: An organized movement to keep me out of any important office.

GRACE: But haven't you always held some important office in the Chapter?

CORNELIA: I have never been *Regent* of it!

GRACE: Oh, you want to be *Regent?*

CORNELIA: No. You misunderstand me. I don't *"want"* to be Regent.

GRACE: Oh?

CORNELIA: I don't "want" to be anything whatsoever. I simply want to break up this movement against me and for that purpose I have rallied my forces.

GRACE: Your—*forces?* [*Her lips twitch slightly as if she had an hysterical impulse to smile.*]

CORNELIA: Yes. I still have some friends in the chapter who have resisted the movement.

GRACE: Oh?

CORNELIA: I have the solid support of all the older Board members.

GRACE: Why, then, I should think you'd have nothing to worry about!

CORNELIA: The Chapter has expanded too rapidly lately. Women have been admitted that couldn't get into a front pew at the Second Baptist Church! And that's the disgraceful truth . . .

GRACE: But since it's really a patriotic society . . .

CORNELIA: My dear Grace, there are two chapters of the Confederate Daughters in the city of Meridian. There is the Forrest chapter, which is for social riffraff, and there is *this* chapter which was *supposed* to have a *little* bit of *distinction!* I'm not a snob. I'm nothing if not democratic. You know *that!* But—[*The phone rings. Cornelia reaches for it, then pushes it to Grace.*]

GRACE: Miss Scott's residence! Oh, yes, yes, just a moment! [*She passes phone to Cornelia.*] It's Esmeralda Hawkins.

CORNELIA [*into phone*]: Are you upstairs now, dear? Well, I wondered, it took you so long to call back. Oh, but I thought you said the luncheon was over. Well, I'm glad that you fortified yourself with a bite to eat. What did the buffet consist of? Chicken à la king! Wouldn't you know it! That is so characteristic of poor Amelia! With bits of pimiento and tiny mushrooms in it? What did the ladies counting their calories do! Nibbled around the edges? Oh, poor dears!—and afterwards I suppose there was lemon sherbet with ladyfingers? What, lime sherbet! And *no* ladyfingers? *What a departure!* What a *shocking* apostasy! I'm quite stunned! Ho ho ho . . . [*She reaches shakily for her cup.*] Now what's going on? Discussing the Civil Rights Program? Then they won't take the vote for at least half an hour!—Now Esmeralda, I *do* hope that you understand my position clearly. I don't wish to hold any office in the

282

chapter unless it's by acclamation. You know what that means, don't you? It's a parliamentary term. It means when someone is desired for an office so unanimously that no vote has to be taken. In other words, elected automatically, simply by nomination, unopposed. Yes, my dear, it's just as simple as that. I have served as Treasurer for three terms, twice as Secretary, once as Chaplain—and what a dreary office that was with those long-drawn prayers for the Confederate dead!—Altogether I've served on the Board for, let's see, fourteen years!—Well, now, my dear, the point is simply this. If Daughters feel that I have demonstrated my capabilities and loyalty strongly enough that I should simply be named as Regent without a vote being taken—by unanimous acclamation!—why, then, of course I would feel obliged to accept . . . [*Her voice trembles with emotion.*]—But if, on the other hand, the—uh—*clique!*—and you know the ones I mean!—is bold enough to propose someone else for the office—Do you understand my position? In that eventuality, hard as it is to imagine,—I prefer to bow out of the picture entirely!—The moment another nomination is made and seconded, my own must be withdrawn, at once, unconditionally! Is that quite understood, Esmeralda? Then good! Go back downstairs to the meeting. Digest your chicken à la king, my dear, and call me again on the upstairs phone as soon as there's something to tell me. [*She hangs up and stares grimly into space. Grace lifts a section of grapefruit on a tiny silver fork.*]

GRACE: They haven't had it yet?

CORNELIA: Had what, dear?

GRACE: The election!

CORNELIA: No, not yet. It seems to be—imminent, though . . .

GRACE: Cornelia, why don't you think about something else until it's over!

283

CORNELIA: What makes you think that I am nervous about it?

GRACE: You're—you're *breathing* so fast!

CORNELIA: I didn't sleep well last night. You were prowling about the house with that stitch in your side.

GRACE: I *am* so sorry. You know it's nothing. A muscular contraction that comes from strain.

CORNELIA: What strain does it come from, Grace?

GRACE: What strain? [*She utters a faint, perplexed laugh.*] Why!—I don't know . . .

CORNELIA: The strain of *what?* Would you like *me* to tell you?

GRACE: —Excuse me, I—[*rising*]

CORNELIA [*sharply*]: Where are you going?

GRACE: Upstairs for a moment! I just remembered I should have taken my drops of belladonna!

CORNELIA: It does no good *after* eating.

GRACE: I suppose that's right. It doesn't.

CORNELIA: But you want to escape?

GRACE: Of course not . . .

CORNELIA: Several times lately you've rushed away from me as if I'd suddenly threatened you with a knife.

GRACE: Cornelia!—I've been—jumpy!

CORNELIA: It's always when something is almost—*spoken*—between us!

GRACE: I hate to see you so agitated over the outcome of a silly club-woman's election!

CORNELIA: I'm not talking about the Daughters. I'm not even thinking about them, I'm—

GRACE: I wish you'd dismiss it completely from your mind. Now would be a good time to play some records. Let me put a symphony on the machine!

CORNELIA: No.

GRACE: How about the Bach For Piano and Strings! The one we received for Christmas from Jessie and Gay?

CORNELIA: No, I said, No, I said, No!

GRACE: Something very light and quiet, then, the old French madrigals, maybe?

CORNELIA: Anything to avoid a talk between us? Anything to evade a conversation, especially when the servant is not in the house?

GRACE: Oh, here it is! This is just the thing! [*She has started the phonograph. Landowska is playing a harpsichord selection. The phonograph is at the edge of the lighted area or just outside it.*]

[*Cornelia stares grimly as Grace resumes her seat with an affectation of enchantment, clasping her hands and closing her eyes.*]

[*In an enchanted voice:*] Oh, how it smooths things over, how sweet, and gentle, and—pure . . .

CORNELIA: Yes! And completely dishonest!

GRACE: Music? Dishonest?

CORNELIA: Completely! It "smooths things over" instead of—speaking them out . . .

GRACE: "Music hath charms to soothe the savage breast."

CORNELIA: Yes, oh, yes, if the savage breast permits it.

GRACE: Oh, sublime—sublime . . .

CORNELIA [*grudgingly*]: Landowska is an artist of rare precision.

GRACE [*ecstatically*]: And such a noble face, a profile as fine and strong as Edith Sitwell's. After this we'll play Edith Sitwell's Façade. "Jane, Jane, tall as a crane, the morning light creaks down again . . ."

CORNELIA: Dearest, isn't there something you've failed to notice?

GRACE: Where?

CORNELIA: Right under your nose.

GRACE: Oh! You mean my flower?

CORNELIA: Yes! I mean your rose!

GRACE: Of course I noticed my rose, the moment I came in the room I saw it here!

CORNELIA: You made no allusion to it.

GRACE: I would have, but you were so concerned over the meeting.

CORNELIA: I'm not concerned over the meeting.

GRACE: Whom do I have to thank for this lovely rose? My gracious employer?

CORNELIA: You will find fourteen others on your desk in the library when you go in to take care of the correspondence.

GRACE: Fourteen other roses?

CORNELIA: A total of fifteen!

GRACE: How wonderful!—Why fifteen?

CORNELIA: How long have you been here, dearest? How long have you made this house a house of roses?

GRACE: What a nice way to put it! Why, of course! I've been your secretary for fifteen years!

CORNELIA: Fifteen years my companion! A rose for every year, a year for every rose!

GRACE: What a charming sort of a way to—observe the—occasion . . .

CORNELIA: First I thought "pearls" and then I thought, No, roses, but perhaps I should have given you something golden, ha ha!—Silence is golden they say!

GRACE: Oh, dear, that stupid machine is playing the same record over!

CORNELIA: Let it, let it, I like it!

GRACE: Just let me—

CORNELIA: Sit down!!—It was fifteen years ago this very morning, on the sixth day of November, that someone very sweet and gentle and silent!—a shy, little, quiet little widow!—arrived for the first time at Seven Edgewater Drive. The season was Autumn. I had been raking dead leaves over the rose-bushes to protect them from frost when I heard footsteps on the gravel, light, quick, delicate footsteps like Spring coming in the middle of Autumn, and looked up, and sure enough, there Spring was! A little person so thin that light shone through her as if she were made of the silk of a white parasol! [*Grace utters a short, startled laugh. Wounded, Cornelia says harshly:*] Why did you laugh? Why did you laugh like that?

GRACE: It sounded—ha ha!—it sounded like the first paragraph of a woman's magazine story.

CORNELIA: What a cutting remark!

GRACE: I didn't mean it that way, I—

CORNELIA: What other way could you mean it!

GRACE: Cornelia, you know how I am! I'm always a little embarrassed by sentiment, aren't I?

CORNELIA: Yes, frightened of anything that betrays some feeling!

GRACE: People who don't know you well, nearly all people we know, would be astounded to hear you, Cornelia Scott, that grave and dignified lady, expressing herself in such a lyrical manner!

CORNELIA: People who don't know me well are everybody! Yes, I think even *you!*

GRACE: Cornelia, you must admit that sentiment isn't like you!

CORNELIA: *Is nothing like me but silence?* [*The clock ticks loudly.*] *Am I sentenced to silence for a lifetime?*

GRACE: It's just not like you to—

CORNELIA: Not like me, not like me, what do you know what's like me or not like me!

GRACE: You may deny it, Cornelia, as much as you please, but it's evident to me that you are completely unstrung by your anxieties over the Confederate Daughters' election!

CORNELIA: Another thinly veiled insult?

GRACE: Oh, Cornelia, please!

CORNELIA [*imitating her gesture*]: "Oh, Cornelia, please!!"

GRACE: If I've said anything wrong, I beg your pardon, I offer my very humble apologies for it.

CORNELIA: I don't want apologies from you. [*There is a strained silence. The clock ticks. Suddenly Grace reaches across to touch the veined jewelled hand of Miss Scott. Cornelia snatches her own hand away as though the touch had burned her.*]

GRACE: Thank you for the roses.

CORNELIA: I don't want thanks from you either. All that I want is a little return of affection, not much, but sometimes a little!

289

GRACE: You have that always, Cornelia.

CORNELIA: And one thing more: a little outspokenness, too.

GRACE: Outspokenness?

CORNELIA: Yes, outspokenness, if that's not too much to ask from such a proud young lady!

GRACE [*rising from table*]: I am not proud and I am not young, Cornelia.

CORNELIA: Sit down. Don't leave the table.

GRACE: Is that an order?

CORNELIA: I don't give orders to you, I make requests!

GRACE: Sometimes the requests of an employer are hard to distinguish from orders. [*She sits down.*]

CORNELIA: Please turn off the victrola. [*Grace rises and stops the machine.*] Grace!—Don't you feel there's—*something unspoken* between us?

GRACE: No. No, I don't.

CORNELIA: I do. I've felt for a long time something unspoken between us.

GRACE: Don't you think there is always something unspoken between two people?

CORNELIA: I see no reason for it.

GRACE: But don't a great many things exist without reason?

maker predispose me toward anything but wayward kinds of love-seeking?

GRACE: —I thought we agreed that all of that is of no consequence now.

HART: While I existed, yes, it did mean much, if not everything.

GRACE: —Granted, it's all absolved and forgotten nearly but—

HART: Then can we continue this obvious impossibility, a talk between us, on a quiet level? I paid very dearly, Grace, to rest upon a quiet level. Will you please not take it from me, will you—

GRACE: Hart, please, that frigid attitude, now, at my—

[*Wind and sea sound, vast and heavy, subside before words resume.*]

HART: At your what, Grace?

GRACE: My—distance. Away.

HART: The question isn't affected at all by distance and can't be fairly called frigid since my concern for you, Grace, was—

[*Sound*]

GRACE [*overlapping*]: *Your concern for?*

HART: *My concern for you, Grace.*

GRACE: Your *concern* for me, Hart?

[*She laughs desperately, bitterly.*]

HART: There again—

GRACE: Again?

HART: You prefer to dismiss it and to mock it although I'm sure you still know—

GRACE: Sure that I still know what?

HART: That my concern for you, Grace, was central to my being as the heart of my body.

GRACE: If those bones thrown and scattered on the ocean's floor, like a gambler's dice, as you said, have in them no blood of mine, then how could they have a heart in them whose central concern is with me?

HART: You can't seem to believe that now I can only speak of what was, not of what is.

GRACE: What was—no matter what the distance and depth of the sea dividing us now—is still what it was, preserved—

[*Sea sound*]

—imperishably.

HART: You and dear grandmother, Grace, not only sold the house on Euclid in Cleveland but the place on the Isle of Pines.

GRACE: The place on the Isle of Pines would have been lost to Cuba, and as for the Cleveland place on Euclid, Mother Elizabeth and I were forced to sell it to go to Florida, Hart.

324

HART: I was left no place. A poet must have a place. When I begged the candyman in Cleveland to give me a loan to buy a small house, he wrote me back that his chocolate business had steadily declined since 1922 and that his new enterprise, that Cozy Country Inn, Canary Cottage in Chagrin Falls, had only possible profits in a dubious future. Still—his stinginess with me, like so much else that mattered when I existed, is irrelevant to me now—is dismissed by the judge in the big, the immense empty courtrooms of such a long time away.

GRACE: Chocolate business in Cleveland and Cozy Country Inn, Chagrin Falls: suitable monuments to a man who wrote such cheerfully vacuous letters, refusing appeals from his son, who was constructing a myth of America, far beyond the reach of the chocolate stained fingers of his—complacent small mind.

[*Sea sounds: her voice comes out of them, crying out.*]

I sold my beautiful diamonds for a song! Do you know what I was finally employed at?

HART: And the house in Cleveland and the place on the Isle of Pines. But are these the things we have to say to each other across the depth and distance, an impossible distance. —Didn't you start to tell me what you're now employed at, what you're working at now?

GRACE: Till recently: not now. Now what I'm employed at—

HART: What?

GRACE: That which you must have suspected since first you heard my voice over this tenuous connection that must break off in a moment and never be restored. I have made it my dedication, my vocation, to protect your name, your legend, against the filthy scandals that you'd seemed determined to demolish

325

them with. Despite my age, my illness, I have carried the stones to build your tower again. And it did hurt me, Hart, that you wrote of the lovely little things such as the flowers of Mexico, carried in woven straw baskets on Indian women's heads under your windows in Pueblo, the bravely common bright flowers of which you wrote in a letter *not to me*—the violets, cornflowers, white and red carnations, the carmine poppies—[*Then savagely*] A wire to you, I quote: COME AT ONCE DESPERATELY ILL AT HOME ALONE YOU CAN HELP. Close quote. Did you? Did you come to me, *did* you help?

[*Rise of sea sound*]

HART: —I—enquired of—friends in Cleveland—if the appeal was—if the circumstances were—authentic—

GRACE: Before that I wired you from California, Quote: MOTHER PASSED AWAY TONIGHT FUNERAL HERE ADVISE. Close quote. If you replied, the letter does not survive!

HART: I appealed to father to give you assistance, to make some provision for your—welfare, Grace.

GRACE: —I wonder if what you confessed in California, that obscene confession of your sexual nature hasn't a little to do with so much of such well-demonstrated grace of the heart in you, Hart.

[*Sea sound*]

HART: What have you been employed at? This time, please, no evasion!

[*Pause: sea sound and music*]

GRACE: I've been employed at nights as a scrubwoman, Hart.

326

HART: —As a—?

GRACE: *Night! Scrub! Woman!*

HART: *Oh—Grace! No!*

GRACE: It's of no consequence, now, but that was my last employment. —Traveller, stranger, son—my friend . . .

[*She closes her eyes and steps back from the lectern.*]

HART [*more and more faintly but with anguish*]: Grace—Grace—Grace—

[*His repeated calls are lost in sea sounds and music: he closes his eyes, which the Mexican painter Sequiras could only paint closed, as they contained such torment, and steps back from the lectern.*]

THE END

THE DEMOLITION DOWNTOWN

Count ten in Arabic—and try to run

CHARACTERS

MR. LANE

MRS. LANE

MR. KANE

MRS. KANE

ROSEMARY (a child)

GLADYS (a child)

THE DEMOLITION DOWNTOWN

The play is set in an upper-middle-class living room on the out-skirts of a capital city.

At the curtain's rise an attractive, youngish man is staring tensely downstage. After some moments his wife lets herself in the front door of the house, stage right or left. She is also youngish and attractive. They are Mr. and Mrs. Lane. Scattered throughout the play are the sounds of dynamite blasts and fall-ing walls of buildings, sometimes alarmingly near.

MRS. L.: No luck.

MR. L.: Why didn't you let me know you were going out?

MRS. L.: You were upstairs. I thought you might be taking nap.

MR. L.: How could you imagine I'd be taking a nap?

MRS. L.: I suppose I'm not used to your being home before six.

MR. L.: When you came in you said, "No luck." What did you mean by no luck?

MRS. L.: I went to see if the supermarket or Kwik-chek might be open again.

MR. L.: Still closed?

MRS. L.: No sign of life on the premises of either.

MR. L.: I don't want you to go out of the house without letting me know.

MRS. L.: Has the house turned into a jail and are you the war-den of it?

MR. L.: Each of us has to know where the other one is at all times.

MRS. L.: Jeff, I think it's best to act as if nothing has happened.

MR. L.: We mustn't pretend to each other.

MRS. L.: All right, we're anxious, but we don't have to act like criminals, caught and convicted, waiting for execution.

MR. L.: Neither of us leaves the house without.

MRS. L.: I told you why I went out.

MR. L.: I told you we've got to know at all times where.

MRS. L.: Didn't I just tell you why I went out?

MR. L.: When I found you'd.

MRS. L.: Gone about ten minutes to see if.

MR. L.: You'd disappeared from the house and I didn't know where you'd, and anyway we mustn't use the cars. The filling stations are shut down. Did you hear what I said? The filling stations are shut down, so we've got to reserve the gas and oil in the cars for a possible trip somewhere.

MRS. L.: We don't understand what each other.

MR. L.: We might want to go on a, we might decide to. We might want to take a little trip some place while I'm free to do it.

MRS. L.: You mean running away, and where's to run to? Don't you imagine that?

MR. L.: We don't *listen* to each other!

MRS. L.: Don't you imagine that, wouldn't you guess that the highways out of the city are barricaded?

MR. L.: There are roads not traveled on much.

MRS. L.: Do you want to know why I really went out? I really went out because I like, I need the sight of familiar places and, and. Familiar places and things, that's why I went out for ten minutes. It was good for my nerves to go out, and so was driving my car.

MR. L.: Driving a Jaguar sports car when.

MRS. L.: Oh, for the love of!

MR. L.: Hunting trips have taught me where these roads are. Roads unknown to, roads only known to, to a few people only.

MRS. L.: Jeff, for the love of, don't, don't suddenly show me a.

MR. L.: I suppose you.

MRS. L.: A yellow streak in you, Jeff. This isn't the time to.

MR. L.: To use a little precaution is.

MRS. L.: Yes, well just to see them, even shut down, it made me.

MR. L.: See what?

MRS. L.: The supermarket and Kwik-chek. I felt like someone still living a usual, normal sort of.

MR. L.: Fine, but you understand that.

MRS. L.: Oh, God, Jeff, I.

MR. L.: Not reserving the gas and oil in the cars is.

MRS. L.: Okay, okay, Mr. Lane! Get me a donkey! An old one, a mangy old donkey! For transportation! But I will *not* stay in *always!*

[*She snatches a gin bottle from the bar.*]

MR. L.: —How much is left in?

MRS. L.: About a couple of fingers. Do we have to reserve it or can we dissipate now?

MR. L.: Let's have it now. I didn't mean to shout at you.

MRS. L. [*as she shakily pours the gin in two glasses*]: No dry vermouth left, baby.

MR. L.: Baby, take off your hat. [*The request is ignored. In hat, coat, handbag in her lap she sits beside him on a sofa. The drink calms them down a little.*] Baby, will you at least take off your gloves?

MRS. L.: Gee. Drinking with my gloves on. [*She removes one of the gloves. He removes the other.*]

MR. L.: Where did you leave the Jaguar, in the garage or?

MRS. L.: I left it in front of the house.

MR. L.: Give me the key and I'll put it in the garage.

MRS. L.: There's nothing top secret about it.

MR. L.: I said please give me the key to the Jaguar, baby.

MRS. L.: I don't have the key; I don't know what I did with it.

MR. L.: I think you probably left it in the.

MRS. L.: Yes, probably, yes.

MR. L.: It's all right, baby, I'll.

[*He goes out. She finishes her drink and takes a sip of his. There is a particularly loud dynamite blast. It changes the angles of the pictures.*]

MRS. L.: Lord God in the—*Highest!* [*As Mr. L. comes back in:*] Didn't it feel good to go out for a minute?

MR. L.: What?

MRS. L.: I didn't say anything. There ought to be a reassuring statement to the people anytime now.

MR. L.: Barbarians don't, won't, can't reassure.

MRS. L.: I've heard that he comes from the intellectual class, and has a degree in—

MR. L.: Yes, in a pig's—

MRS. L.: . . . in law.

MR. L.: In violation of law and in destruction of order and disruption of—. TV dead. Radio dead. Newspapers not delivered since he seized the—

MRS. L.: Don't say "seized." Say "took over."

MR. L.: Take off your hat and coat, and put your handbag down; you're in the house.

MRS. L.: There'll be something, there has to be just something, or.

MR. L.: It's a week and a half and there's been nothing but—nothing.

MRS. L.: Any day there'll be a—

MR. L.: There'll be what? I don't expect anything.

MRS. L. [*taking off her coat*]: Isn't it lucky we have so much in the deep-freeze, Jeff?

MR. L.: Yes, since otherwise we'd. —Honey, do you know that you're still holding your handbag?

MRS. L.: —Of course I don't mind, Jeff, but the fly of your pants isn't zipped.

MR. L.: —Oh. Sorry. [*He zips the fly.*] I suppose that.

MRS. L.: Under the circumstances.

MR. L.: We have to make allowances for.

MRS. L.: I think we ought to make love, right now, on the sofa.

MR. L.: Thank you, honey, but anxiety and lovemaking? You'd find me disappointing.

MRS. L.: That's something I've never found you anytime, Jeff.

MR. L.: A man has a nervous system that has to be prepared for lovemaking, in the right gear for it, and.

MRS. L.: I was thinking of what might be a pleasant distraction for us.

MR. L.: Let's think of it after the blasting quits for the day.

MRS. L.: All right. I'll remind you later.

MR. L.: Yes. Later. Upstairs.

MRS. L. [*suddenly calling out*]: Sally!

MR. L.: Honey, the maid hasn't been here since the blasting began.

MRS. L.: Gee. Yes. Didn't show up for her payday. Well— [*Sound of more blasting.*] I'm glad that Rosemary and Gladys are at Sacré Coeur.

MR. L.: All schools, and Sacré Coeur is a school, have been—

MRS. L.: —What?

MR. L.: Converted to—

MRS. L.: What?

MR. L.: Barracks. I heard that from—

MRS. L.: Too many people have been guessing too wildly about too many things, and Sacré Coeur is a convent school, and.

MR. L.: The church and the new government aren't on what I'd call the friendliest terms. Would you say that they were?

MRS. L.: Oh, you seem determined to demoralize us completely when we're already demoralized, Jeff.

MR. L.: I'm not demoralized.

MRS. L.: Then why can't you sit still? Sit on the sofa and let me rub your forehead.

MR. L. [*following the suggestion*]: Not to be slightly disturbed would be— [*Sound of blasting.*] That didn't sound much further than ten or twelve blocks away.

MRS. L.: At first the blasting was only in the morning.

MR. L.: I've found out one thing. Anxiety is the most useless feeling a person can feel.

MRS. L.: I'd say it's a useful feeling, since it makes you aware of circumstances that could be, that might be not quite favorable to you.

MR. L.: Don't leave the house again without letting me know.

MRS. L.: —Jeff, in a marriage that's been as good, remarkably good, as ours has always been till just now, there shouldn't be orders. Should there?

MR. L.: Honey, don't you think it's wise to reserve the.

MRS. L.: Gas and oil in the cars. Okay. —Are we just going to rattle around here picking on each other till we forget that we love each other?

MR. L.: Oh, for.

MRS. L.: Whose sake?

MR. L.: The sake of consideration of.

[*Blasting.*]

MRS. L.: That rattled the windows and shook the Vertes off the wall.

MR. L.: Yes, I noticed it did.

MRS. L.: Wouldn't you think if there's all this.

MR. L.: —Demolition—downtown. [*He hangs the picture up. Immediately there's another blast and the picture is shaken down again.*]

MRS. L. [*tossing the Vertes on the sofa*]: That put the Dufy at a forty-five-degree angle. [*Mr. L. sits down and immediately springs up.*] You couldn't sit still?

MR. L.: I guess not. —You have a little twitch at the side of your mouth today.

MRS. L.: If we didn't show some symptoms of nervous uncertainty we'd be unnatural creatures.

MR. L.: Stop picking up things for no reason, looking at them with a blind look, and setting them back down. It's.

MRS. L.: It's natural for us to—

MR. L.: Not know what we're doing? —House confinement. No activity.

MRS. L.: I make up the beds and I prepare meals and I even dust the furniture and run the vacuum cleaner over the—

MR. L.: Why bother?

MRS. L.: I think we have to keep up some semblance of usual activity or we'll find ourselves climbing the walls. I didn't realize that Sally was such a poor servant till I started doing the housework myself.

MR. L.: Take your hat off, will you?

MRS. L.: I always do that in the bedroom.

MR. L.: Oh. Do you?

MRS. L.: Love, you're shaking, you're.

MR. L.: How could I feel well? Are *you* feeling well? Well, *are* you?

MRS. L.: I feel—

MR. L.: What?

MRS. L.: I always feel energetic and a little high-strung in the fall. Do you know what I think I'm going to do? I think I'm going out in the yard and rake up the dead leaves.

MR. L.: You're not going out in the yard.

MRS. L.: It would be a normal activity.

MR. L.: I think we ought to make the house look unoccupied until the—

MRS. L.: That's what I'm going to do, to work off my nervous energy. [*She goes through an upstage door. He lights a cigarette*

and burns his fingers with the match. She reenters with a rake.]
The front lawn first.

MR. L. [*seizing the rake and throwing through the dark up-stage door*]: The house is not occupied. Get it?

MRS. L.: Not a bit of it. Two lunatics live in it.

MR. L.: That's the goddamn truth. Come here.

MRS. L.: What for?

MR. L.: This. [*He pulls up her skirt and runs his hands over her buttocks.*]

MRS. L.: That's what I suggested. You said you were too nervous.

MR. L. [*feeling the front of his pants*]: Well, I guess I was right.

MRS. L.: I paid you the compliment of taking off my hat and coat in the living room.

MR. L.: Thank you. I'm sorry. The tension won't last much longer.

[*There is a pounding at the door. After some hesitation Mr. Lane unbolts it, opens it a few inches. Two little girls, Rosemary and Gladys, burst into the room. Mr. and Mrs. Lane are curiously indifferent to their homecoming.*]

ROSEMARY: Daddy! Mummy!

GLADYS: Mummy! Daddy!

MRS. L.: Why have you girls left Sacré Coeur?

ROSEMARY: It was captivated.

MR. L.: Do you mean captured?

ROSEMARY: Yes.

GLADYS: Captured.

ROSEMARY: The Sisters and the Mother Superior.

GLADYS: They were hauled away in a truck.

ROSEMARY: We ran and ran.

MRS. L.: You look like you'd been playing in a pile of cinders. Go right upstairs and bathe and go to bed.

GLADYS: Is everything all right here?

MR. L.: Perfectly, perfectly.

MRS. L.: Upstairs. Bathe. Get in bed.

ROSEMARY: A man with a black beard did a nasty thing to us.

MR. L.: What did he—?

MRS. L.: Didn't you hear me? Upstairs, I said, and bathe and get in your beds.

[*The little girls run up a flight of steps to a landing where the steps turn out of sight.*]

MR. L. [*with no real interest*]: They said that they were molested.

MRS. L.: They seemed like—

MR. L.: What?

MRS. L.: Strangers, complete strangers, to me.

MR. L.: Sacré Coeur's shut down.

MRS. L.: The nuns and that horsefaced Mother Superior hauled away in a truck. Oh. —I took a steak out of the deep-freeze this morning.

MR. L.: Oh.

MRS. L.: Yes. And some lima beans.

MR. L.: Until there's some explanation, I think we should eat in the kitchen by candlelight.

MRS. L.: Eat anywhere you want to, but I'm not going to live in a dark house, Jeff.

MR. L.: It's time for the news report.

[*He switches on the TV. Its face is blank. It gives off a crackling sound.*]

MRS. L.: An interesting news report.

MR. L.: We have to get out of here. Thank God for my hunting trips. We could—no, I guess we couldn't.

MRS. L.: What did you start to suggest?

MR. L.: Spending a week or two at Blue Lake.

343

MRS. L.: No, we couldn't do that. The hotels at Blue Lake had so much employment trouble that they shut down the first of September.

MR. L.: You know, I think it's possible that the new party in power, after a little preliminary shakedown, may turn out to be a rigid party but not a, not a—party that lacks human feelings.

MRS. L.: Jeff, I see your point, but the confiscation of your office building wasn't the most reassuring thing in the world. —Would you say that it was?

MR. L.: That could be more temporary than final, baby. [*The sound of a loud blast.*] The blasting sounds closer today.

MRS. L.: Maybe, baby, that's just because you're more disturbed by it today.

MR. L.: I'm naturally somewhat concerned by it but I'm not what you'd call—what did you say? Disturbed? I'm not disturbed, just waiting with concern.

MRS. L.: Is there a difference between being concerned and disturbed?

MR. L.: Disturbed is when you're sweating.

MRS. L.: You're sweating, baby. A little. Like after a hard game of tennis with a hot sun on you.

MR. L.: Do the present conditions of things make you feel nice and cool, baby?

MRS. L.: Me? I'm not thinking of me. [*She sticks her hand in his pocket.*] I'm a pickaninny. Have you got a nickel in your pocket for me to buy a licorice stick or a little bag of gumdrops?

344

MR. L.: Upstairs. Later, baby.

[*The doorbell rings.*]

MRS. L.: —Should we?

MR. L.: Yes, of course, why not.

MRS. L.: I can think of several reasons but not good ones.

MR. L.: See who's at the door, baby. Ask before you open.

MRS. L. [*approaching the door and calling out*]: Who's there?

FEMALE VOICE: Us.

MALE VOICE: Just us.

MRS. L.: Who's us?

MR. L.: Yes, I'd like to know that.

MALE VOICE: The *Kanes*.

MR. L.: The *Kanes*.

FEMALE VOICE: Don't keep us freezing out here.

MR. L.: Baby, let the Kanes in.

MRS. L.: Just a moment. I'm having a little trouble with the new bolt. Ah, there now, come in, come in, how wonderful to see you.

[*Mrs. Lane admits a pair of neighbors, Mr. and Mrs. Kane. They are the same age as the Lanes and similar to them in appearance.*]

MRS. KANE: We haven't seen you since.

MR. L.: Well, hello there, Henry.

MR. KANE: How are you doing, Jeff?

MRS. L.: Sit down, sit down.

[*The Kanes sit down: their nervousness is apparent.*]

MR. KANE: We should have phoned, but Elaine says the phone isn't working.

MRS. L.: Neither is ours.

MR. L.: Henry, how are things at the Bolster Trust?

MR. KANE: Oh, fine, I guess fine, but I, uh, haven't been down there lately.

MR. L.: Any particular reason?

MR. KANE: I thought I'd stay away till things settle down.

MRS. L.: I'm looking to see if there's any liquor and there isn't any except a bottle of sweet vermouth.

MR. KANE: We would have brought some over but we've drunk our little bar dry.

MRS. L.: We've been drinking more than usual since—

MR. L.: Since President Stane surrendered to the, uh.

MR. KANE: New regime.

MR. L.: Yes. Treasonous.

MRS. L.: We might as well drink the vermouth.

MRS. KANE: Yes. Wonderful.

MR. KANE: —Yes. [*To his wife:*] Take your coat off, honey.

MRS. KANE: It's too chilly. I'll leave it on.

MR. KANE: It's not chilly in here.

MRS. KANE: It was so chilly outside. I'll leave my coat on for a while.

MR. KANE: I'm not going to argue with you.

MR. L.: How's your kids?

MR. KANE: Snug as bugs in their beds.

[*Mr. Kane coughs.*]

MR. L.: That's a bad cough you've got there.

MRS. L.: I hope you haven't caught the new virus thing that's been going around.

MR. KANE: It's a bronchial thing, not serious but stubborn, and Dr. Brad's office is closed.

MRS. KANE: We called on the Paynes.

MR. L.: On who?

MR. KANE: *You* know the Paynes.

MR. L.: Oh, yes, sure, the Paynes. How are the Paynes doing?

MRS. KANE: Nobody answered the door.

MR. L.: They were probably out.

MRS. KANE: I don't think they were in.

MRS. L.: People stay in too much, now.

MR. L.: Hmm.

MR. KANE: Elaine here thinks we ought to drive out to Blue Lake.

MR. L.: I was thinking about that, too, and I know an unpaved road that goes to it.

MRS. KANE: It was you that brought up that subject and the hotels on Blue Lake are all shut down till the middle of May.

MR. KANE: We have a wonderful set of camping equipment that I've put in order.

MRS. KANE: Yes, just in case.

MR. L.: We've got a set, too, and I've got it ready, in case.

MRS. L.: We have a lot of tinned goods. You know, sardines and anchovies and.

MR. L.: Salmon and tuna fish and pate and.

MR. KANE: We've got a stock of that, too.

MRS. KANE [*wryly*]: Yes, a big sack of it, in case of sudden hunger on some excursion or other.

MR. L.: I know what you mean. Essentials.

MRS. L.: It's hard to know what essentials are, exactly.

MR. L.: Essentials are what you discover unexpected need of.

MR. KANE: Such as tinned goods and vacation clothes.

MRS. KANE: Fleece-lined coats and jackets.

MR. KANE: And spare tires in good condition.

MRS. KANE: That's right. In perfect condition.

MR. KANE: There's a cold snap tonight.

MRS. KANE: With the harvest moon shining.

MR. KANE: This is the most unpredictable time of the year.

MR. L.: Unpredictable. Yes.

MR. KANE: Completely. I know what you mean.

MRS. KANE [*winking at Mrs. L.*]: So did I. If I got this hand at bridge, I'd indicate once to my partner and let him take it from there. [*Mr. Kane laughs nervously.*] Of course I'm no good at bridge.

MR. KANE: You're pretty damn good at poker.

MR. L.: It's been too long since we've had a good game of poker.

MRS. KANE: That's right. It seems ages.

349

MR. L.: Yes, it seems ages and ages, but we've all been a little distracted.

MRS. KANE: A little at least.

[*There is a pause.*]

MR. KANE: What is an abattoir, Jeff?

MR. L.: An abattoir? An abattoir is a sort of a slaughter pen.

MRS. L.: Only for animals?

MR. KANE: Yes, of course, but old Hugh Wayne received a notice that said, "Kindly present yourself tomorrow, before five p.m. to the Municipal Abattoir. If you disregard this summons, a squad car will pick you up." He showed me this card, this summons, the day he got it, and he's—

MR. L.: —Not?

MR. KANE: Been seen around since.

MR. L.: We only had the barest speaking acquaintance with old Hugh Wayne. [*A dynamite blast rattles the windows.*] Hmm.

MR. KANE: Hmm.

MRS. L.: Hmm.

MRS. KANE: The closest one yet.

MRS. L.: It was the *strongest* one yet.

MR. KANE [*abruptly*]: The mountains!

MR. L.: What about the mountains?

MR. KANE: We could go to the mountains! Why don't we go to the mountains?

MR. L.: I hadn't thought of the mountains but there's the mountains to go to. And there's the Sunny Peak Road that almost nobody knows of. Two cars?

MR. KANE: One car!

MR. L.: Yes, we could all fit in one car, not too comfortably, but.

MRS. L.: Let's think about it, first.

MRS. KANE: It should be regarded as an idea before it's accepted as a decision.

MR. KANE: You girls are too nervous.

MRS. KANE: You boys are nervous, too.

MR. KANE: We've got the responsibility of decisions.

MRS. KANE: Your wives don't have that responsibility, too?

MR. KANE: Men make decisions.

MRS. KANE: Excuse me for interrupting that male prerogative for a.

MR. KANE: Mountains!

MR. L.: Mountains!

MR. KANE: Let's decide it right now.

MR. L.: Going to the mountains by the Sunny Peak Road. Hard on the rubber, but.

MR. KANE: Siphon the oil and gas in your Mercedes or our Caddy.

MR. L.: When?

MR. KANE: Now, what's wrong with right now?

MR. L.: Nothing that I can think of is wrong with an immediate little.

MR. KANE: What do you girls think?

MR. L.: Yes, how do you girls feel about it?

MRS. KANE: I think it's an inspiration.

MRS. L.: So do I.

MR. KANE: Well, let's get the siphoning going. Now, right now. [*To his wife:*] Turn off the lights while we go out the door.

[*Mrs. Kane extinguishes the living room lights. The door is heard opening and shutting.*]

MRS. KANE: They're out, now. We can turn the lights back on.

MRS. L.: Oh. Yes. Of course. [*The stage is fully lighted again.*] —To get to the Sunny Peak Road, wouldn't we have to go out some fairly well-known highway?

MRS. KANE: I think it might be reasonable to suspect so.

MRS. L.: Wouldn't there, mightn't there be some obstruction, some?

MRS. KANE: If that possibility occurred to our masterminds, it didn't seem to disturb them.

MRS. L.: —No, it didn't, did it?

MRS. KANE: No, it didn't.

MRS. L.: Perhaps they thought about it but—

MRS. KANE: What?

MRS. L.: Knew how to get around it.

MRS. KANE: Yes, that could be the reason they didn't care to discuss it in our presence.

MRS. L.: They don't want us to be nervous. [*A dynamite blast shakes all of the pictures off the walls.*] I'm not going to hang those pictures up again.

MRS. KANE: No, I wouldn't bother. [*Slight pause.*] What do you really think about this excursion to the mountains?

MRS. L.: It's a wild idea, but none of us thought of anything else.

MRS. KANE: The plan is to drive to the foot of the mountains, then get out of the car.

MRS. L.: And go on from there on foot.

MRS. KANE: How good are you at mountain climbing, through several feet of snow?

MRS. L.: —I've had no experience at it.

MRS. KANE: Neither have I, none at all, whatsoever.

MRS. L.: It's a desperate thing to consider, but.

MRS. KANE: The children would be better at it than we'd be.

MRS. L.: Hmm?

MRS. KANE: Hmm . . .

[*Her eyes narrow: she puts on a pair of heavy shell-rimmed glasses which give her a look of cold sagacity: she peers through them at Mrs. L.'s face which is slowly accumulating an expression of shock.*]

MRS. L.: —Hmm!

MRS. KANE: Yes.

MRS. L.: Oh, but, uh—

MRS. KANE: What "uh"?

[*Mrs. L. utters a startled, single-note laugh of incomplete disbelief. On this cue, the little girls are heard singing upstairs the marching song of the guerrilla forces which have seized the capital. Tune: The Battle Hymn of the Republic.*]

GIRLS [*singing*]: "We are crouching in the mountains where the mighty eagles fly, we are waiting in the caverns that are close up to the sky—"

MRS. KANE: The marching song of the guerrillas. Our girls know it, too, and I've learned it from them.

MRS. L. [*rushing to staircase*]: GIRLS! STOP THAT!

MRS. KANE [*slowly, fiercely*]: We can't stop them, you know. Children are creatures that know without knowing, they instinctively know without thinking or knowing, and I think that they know, well, I *know* that they know that siphoning gas out of one car into another is not a true solution and salvation. And, oh, they know we're not old, we're just a lot older than they are, and a generation gap is now a—wide—perpendicular—chasm!

MRS. L.: But they're dependent on—

MRS. KANE: Not us, now. ·

MRS. L.: Oh, but they—

MRS. KANE [*rising*]: The agile, light-footed creatures would glance back once at their clumsy, stumbling parents, maybe call back twice, but soon they'd disappear.

MRS. L.: If we lagged behind?

MRS. KANE: The innocence of savages gives them unlimited visas, expiration date open, valid at any frontier, coming or going. . . . [*She removes her heavy-rimmed glasses, brushes fallen plaster off her coat.*] I think they know without knowing that we are just an encumbrance.

MRS. L.: Oh, Elaine!

MRS. KANE: Hmm?

MRS. L.: We mustn't think, we mustn't—talk like this!

355

MRS. KANE: Get with it, Jane.

MRS. L.: Oh, but—what?

MRS. KANE: About?

MRS. L.: Us!

MRS. KANE: For myself, I have a different plan, I have something else in mind.

MRS. L.: Another idea than?

MRS. KANE: Yes. Totally. In fact, I'd already made a decision before we came here. That's why I've kept on my coat, this plain gray coat. I have nothing on underneath it. Henry said, "Honey, take off your coat, why don't you?" And I said, "I feel cold, dear." Do you want to know my plan?

MRS. L.: Yes, I—

MRS. KANE: You might be interested in it. My plan is to go downtown.

MRS. L.: Are you—?

MRS. KANE: Serious? Completely. My plan is to go downtown in this plain gray coat and find the headquarters of the general and somehow get to see him.

MRS. L.: What would you—?

MRS. KANE: Get to see him, I said. Open my coat and say, "Take me." I'm counting on his being ravenous for a woman, which I think is likely. Before they took the city, they lived in mountain caves, and the general's still a young man. That's my plan. How does it impress you?

MRS L.: —Any plan, now, is a—wild thing to consider.

MRS. KANE: Does this plan of mine seem wilder than Henry's and Jeff's?

MRS. L.: —No, I—

MRS. KANE: The general has a brother. Handsome. Called "The Panther."

MRS. L.: —I have a plain—*what am I saying?*

MRS. KANE: You have a plain coat?

MRS. L.: Yes, I do. It's right here.

MRS. KANE: Strip off quick. Get into your plain coat. [*After a moment's hesitation, Mrs. L. tears off her clothes and gets into her plain coat.*] I know the marching song. Bolt the front door, the siphoning may be finished. We'll sing the marching song as loud as we can on our way downtown. And look ecstatic over the demolition.

MRS. L. [*breathlessly*]: All right! I'm ready! I'm with you!

MRS. KANE: We'll go out the back door and cut across to the boulevard and—

[*Mrs. L. pauses a moment to look about the room she won't see again. She draws a deep breath: then strides purposefully, determinedly, to the dark upstage door, followed by the "cool" Mrs. Kane. They are no sooner offstage than the biggest blast yet precipitates an avalanche of powdery plaster*

357

from the ceiling of the room. Dead on this cue, Mr. L. and Mr. Kane charge in the front door, panting like foxhounds in hot pursuit. And dead on that cue, we hear the voices of Mrs. L. and Mrs. Kane singing loudly into the diminuendo of quick distance.

MARCHING SONG:

We are crouching in the mountains where the mighty eagles
    fly,
We are waiting in the caverns that are close up to the sky,
But without a note of warning, with no trumpet and no drum,
From the peaks of the mountains, will our hungry legions come,
AND OUR TRUTH WILL MAKE US STRONG!

Recognizing the voices of their wives, Mr. L. and Mr. Kane turn to face each other with terrible surmise: as the voices fade in distance, Mr. L. brushes some plaster dust off Mr. Kane's jacket: a courtesy which Mr. Kane returns as—]

THE CURTAIN FALLS